THE PRINCIPLES AND POWER OF SUCCESS

THE PRINCIPLES AND POWER OF SUCCESS

CHARTING THE PATH TO PURPOSE, EXCELLENCE, AND INFLUENCE

DR. MYLES MUNROE

WHITAKER HOUSE

Publisher's note: This book was developed from the extensive teaching archives of Dr. Myles Munroe and approved by Munroe Global Inc. and Munroe Group of Companies Ltd.

Italics in Scripture quotations indicate the author's emphasis.

The forms *LORD* and *GOD* (in small capital letters) in Bible quotations represent the Hebrew name for God *Yahweh* (Jehovah), while *Lord* and *God* normally represent the name *Adonai*, in accordance with the Bible version used.

THE PRINCIPLES AND POWER OF SUCCESS:
CHARTING THE PATH TO PURPOSE, EXCELLENCE, AND INFLUENCE

Munroe Global
P.O. Box N9583
Nassau, Bahamas
www.munroeglobal.com
office@munroeglobal.com

ISBN: 979-8-88769-453-5 • eBook ISBN: 979-8-88769-454-2
Printed in the United States of America

Whitaker House
1030 Hunt Valley Circle
New Kensington, PA 15068
www.whitakerhouse.com

Library of Congress Control Number: 2025943785

1 2 3 4 5 6 7 8 9 10 11 ꟽ 32 31 30 29 28 27 26 25

CONTENTS

PART ONE

THE PURPOSE AND DESIGN OF SUCCESS

1

YOU WERE DESIGNED TO SUCCEED

"Success is knowing your purpose in life,
growing to reach your maximum potential,
and sowing seeds that benefit others."
—John C. Maxwell[1]

E*veryone wants to be successful.* I've never met anybody who planned to fail.

I believe that each human being on earth—no matter what part of the world they live in, what family they come from, what their background is, or what race or nationality they are—desires to be a success. I don't think it's just because they want to be happy or well off or to feel respected by others. I believe it's because everyone in this world was inherently *designed* to be successful. They were not intended to wander around aimlessly in life without direction, and they were not meant to fail at their jobs, businesses, relationships, aspirations, or endeavors.

WHAT IS SUCCESS?

While everyone desires to be successful, they often find success hard to define.

People might name different things that, to them, constitute success. For some, success would mean being financially prosperous; for others, it would mean having popularity, a loving family, or good health; for still others, it would mean overcoming a particular challenge or just surviving in this world. Most of these can be legitimate desires in life, and success might be linked to them. However, do they really define success for us as human beings?

Let me propose to you that since every person was designed to be a success, if we're going to become successful, we must first deal with understanding what that means. We must have an accurate criterion for success. Otherwise, how will we know if we are truly successful?

So, let's go even deeper and ask this question:

Is there ***one definition of success that applies to all humans,*** *regardless of their geographical location, background, gender, age, or circumstances?*

I believe the answer to this question is yes. While success is personal and individual for each one of us, there is still a specific way of measuring it that applies to us all. What it comes down to for every person living on this planet, and what I will describe throughout this book, is that *success means accomplishing the purpose you were put on this earth to fulfill.*

Everything in our life, including our potential for success, is related to our personal purpose. The significance of this is that *following your purpose will inevitably lead to your success.* No matter who you are, you have within you the power to be successful.

You might already consider yourself successful in your chosen field, such as business, law, or education, but you want to learn additional principles for increased success. It could be that you feel successful in one area of your life but want to know how to be successful in other areas as well. Or maybe you have never felt like a success and want to learn the foundational precepts for being successful and prosperous. The principles in this book apply equally to all of these areas; they are principles from which we can continually draw and grow throughout our lives.

Success means fulfilling the purpose that you were put on this earth to accomplish.

MEASURING SUCCESS

In what ways should we measure our success as we follow our personal purpose?

First, success is what you've done compared to what you were designed to do.

We measure our success by our individual calling and abilities. Suppose a bird that was designed to fly has never flown because it has never put forth the effort to do so. That bird has missed its purpose. Yet if the bird spreads its wings and flies because it's the bird's nature to do so, it is successful—it is doing what it was meant to do. Success is first of all discovering what you were born to do, what you were meant to do, and what you are supposed to be doing because of your inherent gifts. Most people have not yet captured what they were born to do. If we haven't been fulfilling our purpose up to now, we may have failed to be successful—but I believe that failure is just postponed success. We can begin to fly in our gifting, no matter what our past.

Second, success means forgetting about competing with others and focusing on pursuing your gift, or your "assignment," in this world.

It is easy to base our success on what others are doing. Yet success is not what we've done compared to what others have done. That's called competition. We'll always find someone who seems to have achieved more than we have—or less than we have. We'll always encounter someone whose skills seem more advanced than ours—or less advanced than ours. Since each person has a personal purpose, it's actually impossible to compare ourselves to anybody else.

One time, when I was growing up, I was very excited because I earned the top mark in my class on an exam. The only problem was, my grade was a 48! That meant that everybody else received a grade of less than 48. When I showed my mother my test, she said, "You got first in the class with a 48? Forty-eight out of what?"

Even though I was at the top of my class with a grade of 48, I had failed the test because the answer to "Forty-eight out of what?" was "100." According to the criteria of the test examiner, even though I received the highest score, I didn't demonstrate that I comprehended the material; in fact, I demonstrated that I had failed to grasp it well. Students may not always receive 100 percent on all their school exams, but, in this context, success may be defined as the fulfillment of the original assignment or purpose for which the test was given.

By what are you evaluating your own success? Success is not about beating someone else in a race. Perhaps you have felt like you were getting by in life in comparison to others, but do you know how you are doing compared to your personal assignment or goal in life? And how do you determine that? In coming chapters, we'll explore how to discover and live out our true purpose and gifting.

SERVING YOUR GIFT

Success means doing everything you can to develop what you were made to do. You don't have to worry about being successful—if you serve your gift, you will succeed!

In this book, I'll explain exactly what I mean by serving your gift. I teach truths and practical guidelines that I have learned over a span of forty-five years, from the time I was a teenager living in poverty and discovering my true potential. My purpose is to equip you with the knowledge and principles necessary for achieving personal development for success. I want to help you to achieve your goals and aspirations, and to fulfill the plan for your life.

There is a lot of information available to us today, but it won't necessarily change our life. We learn a lot of things in the course of a day, a week, a month, or a year that don't actually help us grow and thrive. We need to learn the *necessary things* if we want to be successful. We need to understand principles that will prepare and position us to develop personally, which will lead us to gain the confidence and ability to achieve our plans and goals.

> *You don't have to worry about being successful—if you serve your gift, you will succeed!*

What I am presenting here can turn you into a different person. As you learn what it means to be successful, you may be introduced to yourself for the first time. You might even actually surrender to yourself if you have been avoiding for years what your inner being has been telling you about yourself.

As we explore what it means to be successful, and how that relates to our purpose, it's essential to look at the top five questions in life that every person must consider. These questions serve as the foundation for our success.

2

THE TOP FIVE QUESTIONS IN LIFE

"To be what we are, and to become
what we are capable of becoming, is the only end of life."
—Robert Louis Stevenson[2]

All of human life can be reduced to five questions. These are the ultimate questions of our existence, and they summarize everything about human beings. These questions control the human race; they are so powerful that they motivate everything people do on this planet.

Every issue a human faces is related to these questions because our attempt to find the answers to them leads to our behavior—whether that behavior is positive or negative. People answering these questions in a nonconstructive or negative way is the source of all our problems personally and corporately, in our society and culture: the source of all crime and corruption, broken homes, poverty, war, and much more.

You may have heard these questions posed in other contexts, but for you to be successful in life, you must eventually be able to answer them for yourself. At one time or another, probably every human being on earth has thought about these five key ideas. You are likely reading this book because you've been asking one or more of these questions. The topics we'll discuss in coming chapters contain principles that help us to answer them.

1. *"Who am I?"* This is a tough question. Many people have never answered this question—or even asked it—because it's overwhelming to them or they're even afraid of it. The question "Who am I?" is a matter of *identity*. Many of us still struggle with self-identity. That is why most of us are "other people." Here is what I mean: when we have no established identity for ourselves, we may follow the lifestyles of others in order try to imitate the way those individuals present themselves. For example, we don't wear "ourselves"; instead, we like to wear clothes with the labels of fashion designers or sports figures. These labels reflect certain well-known people. If we lack a sense of our own identity, we may want to be like them. We put on other people's identities in order to feel important. Much of the fashion industry is built on people's lack of self-identity. It feeds on that lack by selling other people's images.

Some people join organizations or even gangs, taking on a group culture because they're trying to find their identity. There's nothing wrong with wanting to have a nice appearance, and it's good to find a healthy community to be a part of, but one of the signs that we're battling with the idea of identity and have lost our true self is that we look or act like other people and end up being someone other than who we really are.

The same applies in relation to our vocations. If we lack self-identity, we may go into a field or take a job simply because of others' expectations of us: perhaps we think our family wants us to pursue a certain position, or a guidance counselor said that's where there were openings in the job market, or our friends decided to work for a certain company, so we did the same.

We don't realize that we're hurting ourselves when we attempt to be like someone else or when we imitate the paths of other people or try to please others instead of discovering our own inherent identity and calling.

2. *"Where am I from?"* I suspect that 99 percent of the world's population never really answers this question. Most of us think of it in geographical terms: "I'm from the Caribbean," "I'm from Brazil," "I'm from Sweden,"

or "I'm from the United States." Yet the question we are looking at here has nothing to do with one's nationality or geographical location. It is something else entirely. This is a question of *human origin*. The answer has to do with the ultimate source of our being or existence.

If you try to find out where you are from by using your national or ethnic heritage, you will get lost. Here's the problem: you can't know who you are (question number 1) until you find out where you are from (question number 2). And you can't find out where you are from if you don't know who you are. The two questions are interconnected.

3. "*Why am I here?*" This is perhaps the most difficult question most people battle with. Why was I born? Why did I come into this world? Why am I present on this planet? This question is directly tied to the issue of *purpose*. It's also tied to questions 1 and 2. If you don't know where you are from and don't know who you are, you'll never know why you are here.

4. "*What am I able to do?*" This question might be phrased, "What am I capable of?" It is a matter of *potential*. We assess our potential by asking ourselves, "What is my true ability in life?" or "What is my true power in the world?" I believe that a majority of people are living below their ability. In my view, that's why, if someone applies themself just a little, other people call them a genius! That's how low some of the standards in our culture have become.

The problem is that our society often attempts to tell us what we can and cannot do. For example, I've seen that the educational system can be one of our greatest impediments to understanding our purpose if it attempts to judge people's potential solely by their exam results. On a given day, you may take a test, and if you get a C, you may be labeled as an average human. But maybe you just had a bad day. Many successful people on earth, such as Microsoft cofounder Bill Gates, never finished school. These individuals had a vision that went far beyond the standard curriculum and test scores.

The educational system doesn't have the mechanism to truly measure how much you know or the potential that is inside you. That's why I don't really trust any system on earth when it comes to measuring people's worth. You may still be living under the cloud of an exam you took in school twenty years ago. Maybe someone told you that you are not artistic or that you don't have the ability to do math—and you believed them. To this day, you are even afraid of using a calculator.

In the first century, Paul of Tarsus said, in effect, "'Let God be true,' and trust no man."[3] That's why we shouldn't fully depend on anyone else's opinions of us and our capabilities. What others think of us shouldn't impact our perception of ourselves and our abilities. Let me tell you something: you are intelligent. Others can't measure your intelligence. Don't believe limiting comments that people have made to you about yourself. Everyone has unique gifts and abilities, and you are smarter than you know. Don't give up on yourself!

I do not guide my life by whether people like me or approve of me. I do not allow either my culture or my country to determine my value in life. I do not allow anyone else to determine how much I'm worth. Why? I have come to understand my inherent purpose, and I like myself before others meet me! I approve of the inner abilities I have discovered. As I explain in a later chapter, that was one of my greatest discoveries in life. Nobody can take that away from me. This is very important for us all to understand. You and I must be careful not to allow other people to judge who we are and what we can do.

5. "*Where am I going?*" This is a question of destiny. What am I aiming for, and how will I know when I arrive? Where am I headed, now and in the future? We'll cover this question, also, as we progress through this book because the combined answers to these questions form the foundation or framework for success in all areas of life.

> *If you don't know where you are from and don't know who you are, you'll never know why you are here.*

MOVING IN THE RIGHT DIRECTION

Success is not a pursuit—it is the *result* of fulfilling your purpose in life: coming to know who you are, where you're from, why you're here, what you can do, and where you're going. But although success is not something we pursue, it is still a journey. And it is a journey that we will follow for our entire life because our purpose is a lifelong gift. We can't be laid off or fired from our purpose, and our gifting doesn't have a retirement clause. You will have success in increments throughout your life on your way to achieving your ultimate purpose.

Thus, success has more to do with moving in the right direction than coming to a destination. It really is a process rather than an end. When you consider your success to be based on the process you undergo to fulfill your ultimate purpose, then you are what is called "fulfilled," or you fulfill your assignment on earth. You are a success.

3

HOW TO DISCOVER YOUR INHERENT GIFTING

"You may get to the very top of the ladder, and then find it has not been leaning against the right wall."[4]

We have seen that success means discovering what you were designed to do, what you were born to do, what you were meant to do.

Many people starting out in life are basically told to get an education and learn some skills so they can get a good job and pay their bills. They are then to continue this cycle of working at a job and receiving a salary so they can keep paying their bills for forty or fifty years until they die. Even if they raise a family and/or make some contributions to their community during those years, working at a job to pay bills is presented as the inevitable reality of their existence. Unfortunately, many people are living this kind of life—a cycle in which they feel trapped and unfulfilled. Maybe you are one of them.

Of course, we need to be able to pay our bills, but we were not supposed to just work a job and pay bills. Our life is meant to be so much more than that. It is meant to be personally rewarding and beneficial to the lives of others. Then, as we carry out our calling, it will be the means of our prosperity.

Other people have been told that their life goal should be to obtain the trappings of wealth, such as expensive clothes and automobiles. Unfortunately, many of these people's gifts lie dormant within them, waiting to emerge. A trumpet is successful when a musician is able to blow notes through it. If a trumpet is sitting on display in your home, it cannot be said to be successful. It may be polished and look shiny, but it is failing at its purpose. The purpose for which a trumpet is made is not to be displayed but to make music. Similarly, a piano that sits in your home unplayed for thirty years is unsuccessful. Even though it may be beautiful and make your home look distinguished, that piano is not fulfilling its purpose because it was not created to be a decorative piece of furniture. It was created to produce music.

How many people are going through life looking shiny and beautiful but not fulfilling their true purpose? Purpose determines success, so if someone wears expensive clothing but doesn't do what they were born to do, they are simply a well-dressed failure! Or if someone rides around in a new car with all the amenities but isn't exercising their true gifts, they are merely a well-equipped failure! Life is not about how expensive our clothes and car are. What's important in life is whether we are doing what we were created to do. In this way, we can truly live and become prosperous while, at the same time, blessing the world with our contributions. And we discover what we were made to do by recognizing our inherent gifting.

PRINCIPLES OF POTENTIAL

Everyone has one or perhaps two main gifts. To have a successful life in which we are fulfilling the purpose for which we were born, we must discover our primary gifting and learn to deploy it. As we do, we can encourage ourselves with these principles:

- *The gift you were born with is more important than the skills you have.* We are not born with skills—we have to learn them. So, there's something higher than skills, which is our inherent gift.

- *You can never lose what you were born with.* Your gift is always with you. It will outlast your skills and keep moving you along in your life's journey.
- *Your future is not ahead of you—it's inside you.* Because you were born with a gift, or a "seed," the key to your life is to discover, develop, and serve this seed-gift to the world. The gift is there—you just need look for it within you.

FINDING YOUR PRIMARY GIFT

How do you know what you were born to do? How do you identify what is meant to enable you to be prosperous? You can begin by answering the following vital questions. After answering them, think about your answers and notice recurring themes and patterns. When you do, you will identify your primary gift.

1. *"What is my greatest desire?"* What do you envision yourself doing? What do you hope to accomplish in life? What would you like more than anything else?

The issue with many people is that they have grown old in their thinking. Do you remember what it was like when you were a child? Did you believe you could become or do what you imagined yourself becoming or doing? When you expressed these dreams, perhaps people told you, "Stop being unrealistic. Stop daydreaming." Those were dream-killers talking to you. It may have begun with your own relatives: "Go to school and get a job. Don't just study what you feel like studying. Study what will bring you money."

May I suggest to you that who you really are is often the thing you first thought of becoming or doing? That's why you are depressed right now. You are not happy in the job where you're working. You hate Monday mornings because you are doing something that doesn't reflect who you are. Your dreams have been destroyed. Have you ever heard people say, "This job is killing me"? They may be correct, because the stress the job is causing them is giving them high blood pressure. They're not built for that kind of stress, so staying in their job may be jeopardizing their health. But when you find your gift and pursue it, it fills you with life.

Two thousand years ago, Jesus of Nazareth said, "In order to live in My kingdom, you have to reverse your life—you must become like a little child again."[5] So, if you're having difficulty identifying your purpose, it may be because you "grew up" too much. That's why you can't pay your mortgage and you're struggling to pay your other bills. You may have become exactly what other people told you that you are, and your dreams have been buried. Perhaps you're making a living, but you're not making a difference. You are surviving but not impacting the world. So, go back and pick up your childhood dream again. I would like to know this: Who are you, trapped on the inside, screaming for release—held fast by a limiting mindset you learned from your culture or family? If you don't remember any real childhood dreams, look into your heart and see the dreams that are currently there. That's who you are.

When you find your gift and pursue it,
it fills you with life.

2. *"What do I wish for humanity?"* Have you ever asked, "Why doesn't somebody do _______________?" or, "I wish somebody would invent _______________"? That may be your destiny calling to you. Another way to look at it is this: whatever you complain about, you may be born to help fix!

3. *"What is my deepest passion?"* You must find out what you are passionate about. When you are passionate about doing something, you want to be involved in it and keep doing it. That is a good indication of what your gift is.

4. *"What are my natural abilities?"* What obvious talents and abilities do you exhibit? What are you good at? What do you truly enjoy engaging in? What have others told you that you are gifted at doing?

5. *"What do I think about being or doing when I am by myself?"* Normally, it is when you are finally quiet and alone that your gift starts "talking" to you and revealing itself. If you are having trouble determining your gift,

it may be because you are always around other people or watching TV, listening to music, looking at your phone, or browsing the Internet, so that you never have any time to reflect and collect your thoughts. You won't find your gift among your friends, although trusted friends who know us well can help to confirm the gifting we sense within us. Many people in history heard the call of their gift when they were alone. In the biblical record, the great leader Moses was tending sheep by himself in the wilderness when he learned the purpose for his life,[6] and the prophet Elijah was in a cave when he heard God whisper a renewed invitation to his calling.[7]

Most of us have lives that are too noisy. Set aside time to be alone and listen to your heart. Where are you able to listen to your innermost being? For example, how long has it been since you've taken a walk by yourself? Or find another way to be alone. Some of my greatest revelations come when I'm in the shower where it's quiet. No music. No radio. No television. (By the way, be careful of listening to media programs, such as some talk shows, that may talk you out of exercising your gift. Shut them off. They will rob you of your destiny, and they never solve any problems.)

Your prosperity lies where your gift is.

6. *"What would I do even if I weren't paid for it?"* What you were born to do is something that you would do and be happy doing even if you weren't paid for it. People who are effective and change the world never do anything for money alone. They do it because they love it and are passionate about it.

People come to me and say, "Dr. Munroe, I want to do what you do—I want to teach and be a public speaker." I say, "Okay, why not volunteer to teach children?" They respond, "No, no, no; I want to be a public speaker." I just gave them a way to develop their gift: practicing on children. Why practice on them? Because they'll let you know when you make a mistake! Many of us want to start right out being paid for our gift. I started as a volunteer teaching Sunday school. And I taught at multitudes of conferences without receiving compensation for it. During that time, I was focused on refining my gift. If you want to be successful, serve your gift for free. Volunteer so that you can grow and become great. Eventually, you will be paid for what you love to do.

I was talking to one of the IT team members in my organization, and I asked her, "How long have you been working here?" She told me it had been about five or six years. Then she added, "But, you know, for five years before that, I used to work here as a volunteer. One day, they said to me, 'You know what you're doing. Why don't you come on staff?'" Now she's working as one of the leaders in our IT department.

Serve your gift at every opportunity. This is what I have done. The more you serve your gift, the more value you build into it. The day will come when someone says, "You know something? I like what you're doing. We're going to finance your program for the next ten years." They've been watching you. Volunteering can be a great avenue to success and prosperity. Sign up to serve.

7. *"What would I do even if it required personal sacrifice?"* When people find their gift, they're normally willing to sacrifice financially to invest in the idea or in making the idea a reality. When my wife and I first built our organization, we had very little. We shared one car. We used to live with my mother-in-law in one room of her house. We had no money to waste. Are you too proud to live simply so you can save money to invest in your idea? Some people are willing to die to achieve their dream; that's what makes them so powerful. Many successful people have had to sacrifice something because they believed in their idea more than their own security. I'm not saying that we are to be financially reckless and not provide for our family. We will talk more in a later chapter about how to transition from working at a job to embarking on true work. Right now, we are focused on identifying our gift, and the question is, "What are you willing to sacrifice to serve your gift to the world?"

Serve your gift at every opportunity.

8. *"What makes me angry?"* Whatever makes you angry is a sign of what you were born to do or to help change. For example, if seeing young people living on the streets without any direction for their lives makes you angry, your gift is likely to assist such young people in some way. If you become angry because elderly people aren't being given proper care and resources, your gift may well be to help older people obtain what they need for their well-being and dignity. If you are angry because there's a lack of specific products or services in your area, your gift may be to supply those products or services.

My anger at third-world oppression is what led me to my gift; it shaped who I have become, and it prompted me to start organizations that address the impact of this issue. I hate the oppression of people—whether they're Black, white, Asian, or Hispanic. I saw what the influence of colonial powers did to my own mindset, and I said, "I hate this." That's why my passion is to transform followers into leaders. Why? Because we were all born to be leaders, but the colonial powers told people in the third world, "You were born to be slaves."

Many successful people were motivated by anger or indignation. Mother Teresa taught at a high school in India, where she witnessed poverty and sickness. This so affected her that she became determined to help "the poorest of the poor" and started her own order called the Missionaries of Charity. She became internationally known for her selfless humanitarian work and was awarded the Nobel Peace Prize.

What makes you angry? If you are still trying to find your gift, perhaps you aren't angry enough. You will never change what you tolerate. You have to get to the point where you can't stand the way things are anymore and you have to do something to change them. So, to find your gift, look for what stirs you inside.

9. *"What do I wish I could change in/about my country?"* This question is similar to the previous one but is not exactly the same. If you're always thinking about something in your nation that you wish were different, you were probably born to help fix it.

Nelson Mandela dedicated himself to changing his country by working to eliminate the institution of apartheid. He was imprisoned for twenty-eight years for fighting against that institution, and after he was freed, he continued to work for racial equality in South Africa and became president of his country.

It may be that your passion and gifts will lead you to pursue reforms and improvements in your own community and/or nation.

10. "*What would I do if I had limitless money and resources with which to do it?*" What endeavor would you pursue if you had all the money you could want? What project or product or activity or enterprise would you spend that money on? Your answer to that question is what you were born to do. Let me tell you something: if you refine your gift and document what you want to do and begin to develop it, the needed money will come in because somebody else was born to finance your dream. The trouble is, they can't invest in it because you haven't yet begun to exhibit your gift or to refine it in such a way that they can see it or in a manner in which you can present your dream to them.

There is an ancient proverb that makes a powerful statement in this regard: "A man's gift makes room for him."[8] You were designed to be known for your gift. That is where your success lies. You have to consider, "What is my gift? What are my assignments? What is my reason for being here?"

THE ONLY THING THAT IS RIGHT FOR YOU

I hope you will enjoy exploring these ten questions. You may have to dig deep to find some of the answers, but the search will be worth it. I want you to discover your true gift in life. I care about you, and I want you to be a success. I don't want you to fail. I know life can be rough, and I want you to understand the principles of success and to develop the inner reserves to meet life's challenges.

You may have been waiting a long time for success and prosperity. You don't have to be a beggar. You're a great woman or man. You have much more inside you that no one has yet seen. You are not finished. You're still on your way. So, wake up and dust yourself off. Find your gift and pursue it! You will become free from the lies people have told you about yourself—or the lies you've told yourself—about who you are and what you can do.

If you have been on a vocational track that has been financially profitable but ultimately makes you feel empty inside, or if you want to do something else that is truly meaningful to you, I want you to know the truth about yourself because the truth that you know will set you free.[9]

People often need to work through a sequence of thoughts, emotions, and conclusions before they make a decision to take action. There is a simple depiction of that process that helps us to understand the way we think about things. In the following list of statements, start from the bottom statement and work your way up. That is normally how we have to think to become successful—from the bottom up.

I did it.

I will do it.

I can do it.

I think I can do it.

I might do it.

I think I might do it.

What is it?

I wish I could do it.

I don't know how to do it.

I can't do it.

I won't do it.

These are simple statements, but they reflect some complex deliberations. I don't know where you are in the sequence right now. Hopefully, you are not on the bottom, saying, "I won't do what I dream." I want you to arrive at the point where you say, "I *will* do it" so you can eventually say, "I did it." "I will do it" is the second from the top because it means the person is committed to—even willing to die for—what they're going for. Pablo Picasso said, "Action is the foundational key to all success."[10]

> *The truth that you know will set you free.*

Until you find your true calling, you will never be satisfied. Your purpose is the only thing that is right for you. You may be familiar with the saying "The enemy of right is not wrong. The enemy of right is 'good.'" You may think your life is going along fine because you're doing something good—but are you doing the right thing? Are you using your gift to fulfill your unique purpose? We can't allow ourselves to be distracted by good things. If we are doing something good, we may have a job or be contributing on some level, but we have not yet found our true gift.

When you find your purpose and fulfill it, that's success.

PART TWO

THE LAWS OF SUCCESS: FOUNDATIONS

4

LIFE'S LAWS OF SUCCESS, PART 1: SUCCESS IS PREDICTABLE

"Someone's sitting in the shade today because someone planted a tree a long time ago."
—Warren Buffett[11]

Recognizing our inherent gift is a powerful first step, but we also need to understand how to activate that gift. We activate it by employing life's laws of success. Unless we follow these laws, we will be unable to fulfill our true purpose. Everything exists by laws and according to laws. Laws are the glue that holds the universe together.

IT'S NOT MAGIC!

Let me make what might seem like a bold statement: Success is *predictable*—and so is failure.

How can I make that statement? Because, as I wrote above, everything in life was meant to function according to laws, and our response to those laws—positive or negative—makes all of life predictable. You can predict if a person will succeed or fail because of the way life is designed. By "designed," I'm not referring to the systems of a particular culture or society, and I'm not talking about ritual laws. I'm talking about the laws that are built into life.

Therefore, the way you relate to life depends on the laws that you know and put into practice. Learning and following these laws is the secret to success and prosperity.

People spend millions of dollars going to all sorts of seminars and reading all kinds of positive-thinking and how-to-succeed books, and they are still broke and lacking purpose. That's because they don't understand that you can't become successful by using another person's ideas. You need your own revelation of those ideas. They have to become yours. Nothing is your own until you believe it. In the same way, I cannot believe the laws of success for you. I can only encourage you to make them your own and to act on them.

I once met Warren Buffett, one of the wealthiest men in the world. He lives in Omaha, Nebraska, and I was in that city to speak at a church. We happened to meet at a restaurant, where Buffett had come in to buy ice cream, and he was so humble. Whenever you meet someone who is successful, ask them questions. That's exactly what I did with Warren Buffett. His answers contained the same information about success that I had learned over the years. This was another confirmation to me that the laws I have learned are universal and cover a wide range of questions, situations, and issues.

Thus, attaining success and prosperity isn't magic. It has to do with understanding your purpose, discovering your gift, and following the established and proven laws of life. I have not only used these laws in my own life, but I have also taught them around the world. They apply anywhere: they have no regard for people's ethnic background, family upbringing, or culture. They work for anyone who learns them and puts them into practice.

In this section, I lay the groundwork for you to understand the purpose and meaning of life's laws of success—their nature and how they function—so that you can effectively put them into practice with the topics I share throughout this book. Unless we have a good grasp of them, we won't comprehend their importance, and we won't exercise them in the proper manner. Then, in the next section, we will begin to apply them in practical ways by learning what it means to have true work rather than a job or another occupation, and outlining key principles for thriving and being prosperous in our work.

Let's begin by looking at the principles that clarify, step-by-step, the ideas about laws I have just described for you so that they can be established as a foundation for success in your life.

> *The laws of success work for anyone who learns them and puts them into practice.*

PRINCIPLES OF SUCCESS AND PROSPERITY

1. EVERYTHING IN LIFE WAS DESIGNED TO SUCCEED

I didn't always understand this principle because, as I mentioned earlier, I was born into a low-income environment. I was taught that you just have to survive, and I developed a survival mentality. A survival mentality will always be a poverty mentality because, with this mindset, you don't believe you deserve to be prosperous. You can actually become afraid of success. Many people are poor because they are afraid to be wealthy. They are mentally convinced that they don't deserve to be prosperous. They're actually afraid of what they want. Whatever you are afraid of stays away from you. You repel what you reject. To get past this mentality, I had to discover the inherent law that everything in creation was designed to succeed.

That was a paradigm shift for me because it meant rejecting the mindset of my upbringing and the low expectations of my society for what I could be. I even had to be convinced that every human being *wants* to be successful. You must recognize that the desire or hunger in your heart to be a success is natural. Now, that makes life very tough for many people, doesn't it? It is the very source of their depression. Their desire for success discourages them because they know what they want to be, but they don't know how to get there. So, although they hate where they are, they feel stuck. The first step toward addressing that hunger is to affirm that you were designed to succeed. The whole idea is to transform the way you think. Success will not come about until your thinking changes.

2. EVERYTHING IN LIFE WAS DESIGNED TO FUNCTION BY LAWS

The reason everything on earth has laws attached to it is that everything was designed to succeed, and these laws facilitate that success. We are at a great disadvantage unless we make a point of knowing and functioning according to them.

3. LAWS MAKE LIFE PREDICTABLE

Often, the reason people fail is that they think that success is due to luck—and luck is unpredictable. But the laws of life make the outworking of life predictable. You are too valuable to live on chance. Your life is not a game. Wherever you are in life right now is a result of laws that you have implemented—or *not* implemented, either because you don't know them or you aren't applying them.

4. SUCCESS IS PREDICTABLE

As I wrote at the beginning of this chapter, success is predictable because it is controllable in this sense: it is related to life's laws. We may go through challenges and setbacks, but if we keep following the laws of life, we will overcome our difficulties and emerge successful.

5. FAILURE IS PREDICTABLE

It follows that if we ignore or disobey the laws of life, we can predict our own failure. For example, if I uprooted a sapling and left it on top of the ground, can I predict what will happen to that plant? Yes. I can predict its failure to function as it was meant to, and unless I do something to help it, it will dry up and die. But if I plant a sapling in the soil and give it water and nutrients, can I also predict what will happen to it? Yes. I can predict its success. Your life is as simple as a plant, but it's also as complicated as a plant. The laws are simple, but we need to faithfully put them into practice. Otherwise, we will struggle throughout life.

Once more, success and failure in life are not mysterious. They are both related to laws.

6. SUCCESS IS NOT A PURSUIT

This is a very important concept. Most people who "try" to be successful do not end up being successful. Are you trying to be successful? Are you trying to be great? Are you trying to be prosperous? It won't happen. Prosperity will run from you. Solomon, the wisest man who ever lived, indicated that for the one who chases money, money takes wings:

> Do not wear yourself out to get rich; do not trust your own cleverness. Cast but a glance at riches, and they are gone, for they will surely sprout wings and fly off to the sky like an eagle.[12]

It is vital to have dreams for your life, but the more you run after success, the more it runs from you. That is predictable because success isn't found that way. A car doesn't "try" to function well. Just give it what it needs for its engine and its other parts to work, just follow the laws that make cars run, and it will function well. It is the same with our life—we need to provide it with what it needs to function well. So, don't make success your aim. Instead, make it your goal to follow your dream and exercise your gift as you obey the laws of success.

Because of some negative connotations of the word, some people might not like the term *obey* when it comes to following laws. However, it simply means "to follow the commands or guidance of" or "to conform to or comply with."[13] We obey many laws of life every day yet often ignore the laws of success. For example, when you eat a meal, you are voluntarily obeying a natural law that says your body needs nourishment to maintain life. Most people don't ignore that law because they know that obeying it will keep them alive. If they refuse to eat, they jeopardize their health. Similarly, obeying the laws of success will sustain you and enable you to thrive.

7. SUCCESS IS A RESULT

If success is not a pursuit, then what is it? It is a *result* or *byproduct* of following laws. People who are truly successful are simply adhering to certain laws and reaping the results.

LeBron James desired to be the best basketball player he could be, so he followed some laws to make that happen. One time, I heard him being interviewed after a game that the Miami Heat, the team he was then playing for, won by twenty points. The interview went something like this: "How did you do it?" the reporter asked. "Well," he replied, "we had a few days off, and instead of resting, we spent all the time in the gym shooting." On their break, what were LeBron and his teammates doing? Even though they were scheduled off, they persisted in following one of life's laws of success: diligence, or hard work. LeBron was telling us that his success was not something he merely *desired* to pursue; rather, he was concerned with *working a law* in order to obtain a result. Such a mindset is essential for success.

The laws of success will sustain you and enable you to thrive.

IN OUR BEST INTERESTS

The two most common reasons for failure in life are therefore ignorance of laws and disobedience to laws. We need to put in the effort to activate life's laws. Obedience to the inherent laws of life is always in our best interests.

In this sense, we become what we decide to be. What I am today, I actually *made a decision* to become. We must learn to stop blaming other people for our state in life. Others may be responsible for hurting you, which is another topic, but they aren't responsible for who you are or what you become. The only way to correct failure is to start following—or return to following—life's laws.

People keep expecting to succeed when they disregard the laws of success. "Whatever a person sows, this he will also reap."[14] Some of you are reaping things right now that you wish you hadn't planted. Again, generally speaking, whatever we are right now, we made a choice to be, whether we realize it or not. That includes being unfulfilled and unprosperous. But if you're not where you want to be, you can begin today to turn things around.

Since success is a byproduct, once we implement a law, we can rest in the fact that the law will go to work for us, as it did for LeBron James. To go back to the analogy of a plant, once you provide the soil, water, and nutrients, you can't do anything to make that plant grow. Your job is to support the laws of nature, and then growth occurs in the plant by an internal working out of those laws. Is there something with your name on it that has been waiting for you to activate a law so it can come into fulfillment?

In the next chapter, we will explore the framework of the inherent laws of success so that we can build upon them as we continue to look at principles of success and prosperity.

5

LIFE'S LAWS OF SUCCESS, PART 2: DESIGNED AND TESTED

"Vision without execution is just hallucination."[15]

The laws of life have a relational aspect to them, and we need to be aware of this context to fully understand and implement them. I want to share with you one of my favorite illustrations that has helped many people over the years to comprehend this aspect and apply it in a variety of arenas, from leadership to personal relationships. It's an example from the world of manufacturing.

PROTECTING THE IMAGE

A manufacturer puts their name and/or logo on every product they make. So, your shoes have a brand name inside them, and the name may also be stitched on the outside. Your shirt has a label with the company's name on it, and the name might also be featured on the front. Your car has a brand name fixed on the back of it. Your phone has a company name or logo on it.

The name or logo on a product reflects its *image*. Apple Inc. has an image. Microsoft Corporation has an image. Ford has an image. Mercedes-Benz has an image. What's most important for us to understand is that, in the manufacturing process, *the last thing a manufacturer puts on a product is its image*. They place the image on their product only when they consider it finished.

Let me define "finished" for you. I'm talking about products, but, ultimately, I'm going to be talking about the way we are designed as human beings. A manufacturer finishes making their product before selling it. However, the company does not allow a product to leave their manufacturing plant until it has been *tested*. They pay people to test the product to make sure everything about it is working. After this process is complete, the company's image is placed on the item, and then the product is prepared for shipping. In this sense, when you purchase a new product, it's not really brand-new—it's already been used in order to be tested. But only then can it be said to be "finished."

When a manufacturer allows a product to leave the plant, they are so sure the product will work that they include an owner's manual with it that contains a lot of promises. If the product is a phone, the user manual might say, "This device can be used to make phone calls." How do they know that for sure? They have already tested it. "This phone can connect to the Internet." How can they make that claim? They've already tested it. "This phone can send text messages." How can they guarantee it? They've already tested it. "This phone's battery will last for eight hours." How can they be sure? They've tested the battery to confirm its longevity. So again, when the manufacturer puts their image on it, that's a sign that the product is not at the beginning of the manufacturing process but at the very end.

The owner's manual also says, "Do not attempt to operate this product until you've read this manual completely." The manual is simply a collection of laws described by the manufacturer that should be followed by the consumer in order to guarantee that the product will function correctly. These laws are clearly not given to harm the product. They are given to protect it.

Now, at the back of an owner's manual (most people never read that far!), there is usually a page entitled, "Warranty." A warranty explains that the company fully backs its product. It says that if anything goes wrong with the item within a certain amount of time—such as two years—if any deficiency exists, if it doesn't work, then, if you ship it back to them, they will pay for the shipment and repair the item at their expense. They will replace any defective parts with new parts directly from their own inventory. They will either ship the repaired product back to you, or, if necessary, they will replace the item with a completely new one (also having been tested)—all at their expense.

The people who run that company don't know you personally, so why would they spend all that money to have you ship the product to them, have the item repaired, and ship it back to you—or to actually give you a new product? Why are they so dedicated to doing this? They aren't doing it because they like you, so there must be some other motivation for why they're so committed to it. The answer? Because none of it is about you. The company does all of that for their own sake—for their name's sake. They are protecting their reputation in the marketplace because their name is on their product.

The owner's manual even warns you not to attempt to fix the product yourself. In other words, no one should try to fix someone else's product. That's a deep statement. Why? Because the company wants its success to be tied to its name. They know that if anything fails in this product, their entire reputation, the public's perception of their character, may be in trouble. Have you ever heard someone say—or perhaps you've said it yourself—"That company has a bad name," or "That business has a bad reputation"? The success of the product is more important to the company than the cost to fix it so they can preserve their name.

A manufacturer does not allow its product to leave the manufacturing plant until it has been tested.

That's also why a company will voluntarily recall certain products and repair them at its own expense. You might receive a notice from the manufacturer of your car that says something like, "If you purchased this particular make and model of car between this year and that year, bring it back to us, and we will fix it at our cost." The company is thinking, "It may cost us six hundred million dollars, but we don't care because there's nothing more expensive than our name." The success of their product protects their reputation because they have put their name on it, and they have guaranteed that it works.

PRINCIPLES OF SUCCESS AND PROSPERITY (CONTINUED)

How does all this apply to our success? In the previous chapter, the first law we looked at was, "Everything in life was designed to succeed." The eighth law is an expansion of that first law:

8. OUR SUCCESS WAS DESIGNED BY THE CREATOR OF THE UNIVERSE

The Creator of the universe decided to make a "product" called human beings. In this context, I am referring to the Creator as the God of the Bible. It was He who gave us our inherent purpose and gifts as elements of the divine part of our human makeup. He said, "Let us make mankind in our image, in our likeness."[16] When He did this, He indicated, "This product isn't going to be like the birds, the fish, or the other animals. This is going to be a unique product. We're going to put Our name on this one."

The word *image* refers to characteristics. God put His stamp, His image, on us so that we would have His very character. The word *likeness* indicates that we function like Him. So, God made us not just to have His characteristics, or qualities, but also to function as He does. And God never fails. Every human being was created to succeed. God has never created a failure. People fail, but that's not God's purpose and will for them.

The Creator had His own manufacturing plant, and He tested human beings before He put His image on them. That's why the first thing we read that God said about human beings is actually the last thing He said about them in the process of creation: "Let Us make mankind and put Our image on them." This means that you did not begin your life when God created you. God told Jeremiah the prophet, in essence, "Before you were conceived in your mother's womb, I already tested you. If I tell you that your purpose is to be a prophet, I'm not starting at the beginning. I am speaking about what I have already tested. Jeremiah, you *are* a prophet."[17]

Therefore, you can say to others, "What I am, I already am. You just haven't seen it yet. I am going to manifest it." Do you understand the significance of this? This is why I said that a test score can't fully measure our potential—or limit it. And this is why I said we shouldn't judge anyone else's potential. The purpose is built into the product. You came to earth because you are finished. When God released you, you arrived with everything you need to fulfill your purpose in life and be successful.

So allow me to ask you again: "Are you trying to pursue success?" It's not wrong to have dreams. The Creator gave you those. But He also showed you the *way* to success. Success is a result of manifesting what the Creator has placed inside you as you follow His laws, which will enable you to fulfill your purpose.

Earlier, we talked about owner's manuals. Do you read every page of the manual that goes with your refrigerator, your car, your phone, or your television? Probably not! That may be the reason you can't figure out why the product does certain things. The item may have twenty-five functions, but you know only four. That means you are not operating it according to all twenty-five facets of its potential. You are living below the product's ability to assist you. In this sense, you are undervaluing the product.

Some of us do the same thing with our lives and our potential for success. We know only four things: Get up and go to work, come home, eat dinner, go to bed. Get up and go to work, come home, eat dinner, go to bed. Get up and go to work, come home, eat dinner, go to bed. We're stuck in life because we have never heard of or closely followed the laws of creation that will make all the difference for us.

God says, "I can't afford for you to fail, because I have placed My name on you." When I discovered this reality, I became "dangerous." I discovered this law when I was sixteen years old by reading the Creator's Manual, the Bible, and drawing from its laws and principles. The Creator gave us specific laws to help us to better understand His nature and align with His purposes, to guide our relationship with Him and other people, and to enable us to be successful in fulfilling our inherent purpose.

I am the same in my attitude today as I was when I first discovered these principles: strong and bold, with no fear about life. Do you know why? I recognize that God created me, that He designed me to succeed, and that my success is in His best interests. I have learned many laws from the Creator that I have applied to business, finance, leadership, relationships, and other areas of life that enable us to be prosperous and fulfilled, and which are the basis of my books.

You may think that you've already mined the depths of your potential, but you haven't seen anything yet! You're going to manifest all that is in your "hard drive." For the last ten or twenty years, all that people have seen—perhaps all that you have seen—has been the computer monitor and the few things you've displayed on it so far. You have so much more than that already within you!

> *You arrived with everything you need to fulfill your purpose in life and be successful.*

THE END FROM THE BEGINNING

You were not born to figure out a purpose for your life. You were born *with* your purpose. Again, the problem may be that you're afraid of yourself and your dreams because your family or culture or government has told you who you can and can't be. (Or because you have told yourself the limits of who you can be.) But they have no idea what they are saying. Don't get your measure and worth from other human "products," because no one knows a product like its manufacturer. Those other products need to mind their own business and keep their thoughts to themselves because they don't know who you are.

The Creator would not have allowed you to begin unless you were already finished. In the book of Isaiah the prophet, God expressed, "I make known the end from the beginning, from ancient times, what is still to come. I say, 'My purpose will stand, and I will do all that I please.'"[18] What He means is that, when you arrived, your finish came with the beginning. God never places the future of anything ahead of it. Perhaps you've never heard this concept before, yet it's essential to recognize it if you want to understand the nature of success. Remember one of the principles of potential: "Your future is not ahead of you—it's inside you." How can the Creator make known what is yet to come? Because what is yet to come already came!

God put inside you who you really are. He says, "When I show you what's ahead of you, you can see it. I will not allow you to see what does not already exist."

What can we conclude from this? We don't have to try to win in life anymore. We are here because we have already won; we are already successful and just need to manifest that success. Now you can see why I became so confident at only age sixteen. I recognized that I was already the winner. I wasn't supposed to try to win—I'd already won.

King David wrote in one of his psalms, "Take delight in the LORD, and he will give you the desires of your heart."[19] But wait a minute—didn't I just say that God gives us His desires, His purposes? Yes, He does. Our dreams originated with Him. But remember that God has placed His desires for us within our heart. The heart, in this case, means the subconscious mind. God put His plans there because He wants to make sure we find them. As we talked about in chapter 3, all the thoughts, ideas, plans, and dreams that remain consistent within you were put there by the Creator. No matter how many times you may temporarily forget about them, they will always come back into your mind.

Let's go back to what God said in Isaiah: "My purpose will stand, and I will do all that I please." In other words, "This is My purpose for your life. It's already finished it, and it will stand." The word *stand* there doesn't mean that it's standing up. It means it won't go away—it will frustrate you until you do something about it. It means you will never be happy doing anything else. We cannot change what we were born to do and to be, and still be fulfilled and successful. Again, that purpose will always frustrate us until we act on it.

As a matter of fact, God goes on to say, "From the east I summon a bird of prey; from a far-off land, a man to fulfill my purpose. What I have said, that I will bring about. And what I have planned, that I will do."[20] What you are created to be can be suffocated, and you can take it to the cemetery, but it can never be changed. As I said earlier, I believe you are a great man or woman—but what have you settled for in life? Have you allowed yourself to be reduced to a number at your job? Perhaps that is how people perceive you. But that's not the way God sees you. He sees you as someone with divine purpose who is a success.

6

LIFE'S LAWS OF SUCCESS, PART 3: LAWS GUARANTEE FUNCTION

"If the ax is dull and its edge unsharpened, more strength is needed, but skill will bring success."
—King Solomon[21]

There are some people who seem to hate any kind of laws. That's because they don't really understand their purpose: good laws guarantee function and serve to protect. Likewise, the laws of life are given to guarantee our function (success), and they also protect us. Why does the Creator beg us to obey His laws? Because obedience to those laws is always in our best interests.

On many occasions, Jesus of Nazareth talked about the essential nature of the Creator's laws. At one point, when He was talking about living in God's kingdom—the influence of heaven on earth—He said, "The knowledge of the secrets of the kingdom of heaven has been given to you."[22] Those "secrets" He also called "keys": "I will give you the keys of the kingdom of heaven, and whatever you bind [lock up] on earth will be bound [locked up] in heaven, and whatever you loose [unlock] on earth will be loosed [unlocked] in heaven."[23] We may have a key to a safety deposit box with $2 million in it, but because we don't know it, we're living as if we were broke.

Jesus said He was going to give us laws by which we can cause heaven to act on earth on our behalf. You can make things begin to happen, or you can stop things from happening, according to these laws. When you use the keys as they were intended, in whatever you allow, heaven will back you up; in whatever you stop, heaven will back you up.

There is not simply a "key"—singular—to the kingdom. There are *keys*—many of them. Why is this so important? Because Jesus said these keys open up heaven or close heaven. They open up life or close life. In other words, keys determine whether you live a locked-up life or an open life. Whether you fail or succeed.

So, you can open up things or shut down things depending on the keys you obey or disobey. Notice that, in this context, Jesus says heaven will do what you do, which, once more, means that He's telling us that success is not up to God—it's up to us.

If you don't know the keys, you can't put the laws and principles into effect. If you know the keys, you can put them into practice, and God will help you. Why? Because He is a God of laws, and He responds to laws. Again, it is just as with any manufacturer: if you obey the laws of the manufacturer, they guarantee that the product will operate because they support their product.

> *You can open up things or shut down things depending on the keys you obey or disobey.*

The only person who knows the secret to the keys is the one who owns them. Scholars of the Bible tell us that the Greek word translated into English as "keys" in Jesus's statement is "figuratively used in the N. T. to denote power and authority of various kinds." They also tell us that, in the ancient world, "because only a limited number of trustworthy persons carried keys, the image naturally conveyed delegated authority and exclusive access."[24]

Later, Jesus told the religious leaders of His day, "Woe to you experts in the law, because you have taken away the key to knowledge. You yourselves have not entered, and you have hindered those who were entering."[25] This key to knowledge "is the means of attaining the knowledge regarding the kingdom of God."[26]

I may have the key to a car but be unable to use that car because I don't know which car door the key opens. So, I could be among a sea of cars and still be walking because the key I hold has a secret that leads to the right car. I must know the law associated with it.

This leads us to principle number nine:

PRINCIPLES OF SUCCESS AND PROSPERITY (CONTINUED)

9. YOUR SUCCESS IS GOOD FOR GOD

We know that everything God created, He built for success: air, water, sky; fish, birds, mammals; atoms, cells, organs; men, women, children. When a tree grows from a seed, it is really not for the sake of the plant; it's for the sake of the Creator. Therefore, the success of a product is not good for the product—it's good for the manufacturer.

You can say to yourself, "My success is good for God!"

When I discovered this truth, it was one of the things that changed my life. I mentioned how I learned this by reading the Bible for myself as a teenager. When I understood the principle that my success is good for God, I began to "put pressure" on God to fulfill what He had promised. We talked about how a product carries with it the entire credibility of the manufacturer and its name. The Hebrew word for "name" is *seth*, and this term is very significant: "In Hebrew thought a name is never a mere label. It embodies identity, character, authority, memory, reputation, and destiny."[27]

In other words, in Hebrew, the name of a thing *is* the thing. In ancient times, a name was not just a label; it was a representation of character. This is why, when the great leader Moses asked God, "What is your name?" it was a problem for God to answer that question. He told Moses, "Well, 'I AM WHO I AM.' That's what I am."[28] In essence, God was saying, "My name is 'I am' whatever I am at the time." That's the way it's written. If you translate it into English, it doesn't make sense. We ask, "God, what is Your name?" God replies, "It depends on what I am at the time. Call Me that." You fill in the blank depending on what God is for you at that moment.

For example, God doesn't heal people. He *is* Jehovah Rapha, the God who Heals. God doesn't bring peace. He *is* Jehovah Shalom, the God of Peace. God doesn't provide things for you. He *is* Jehovah Jireh, the God Who Provides. Some people talk about wanting to know all the names of God, but that's impossible if He becomes whatever you need Him to be at the time. If you are sick, you don't need money—you need Jehovah Rapha. The person right next to you may need money. God becomes Jehovah Jireh to that person. So you have two manifestations of God's character in the same place.

This same God became flesh and dwelt among us in a person called Yeshua—a name translated as Joshua, or Jesus, a name that simply means "Savior." One time, people asked Jesus, "What is Your name? Who are You?" His answer was, "I've been telling you all along who I am, but you don't believe Me." They said, "No, You confuse us because, on Monday, You say, 'I am the light.' Then, on Tuesday, You say, 'I am the way.' On Wednesday, You say, 'I am the truth.' On Thursday, You say, 'I am the life.' On Friday, You say, 'I am the bread from heaven.' On Saturday, You say, 'I am the living water.' On Sunday, You say, 'I am the resurrection.' Which one are You?" Jesus answered that question by saying, in essence, "It depends on what you need." Jesus is everything you need depending on what you need. He says, "What do you need Me to be? I am that."

Here now is our tenth principle of success and prosperity, which is related to number nine:

10. THE SUCCESS OF EVERYTHING GOD CREATED PROTECTS HIS REPUTATION

We talked about how a manufacturer needs their product to be successful for their own sake in the marketplace. The Creator of the universe built success into creation because the success of everything He made protects or guards His reputation. That's why our Manufacturer doesn't leave our success up to chance, guessing, experimentation, or gambling. He builds laws into our operation so that we don't need to wonder about it.

The Creator loves to maintain His reputation. In the Bible, there is a repeated phrase in relation to God that is a manufacturer's phrase. In various places, we see it expressed as "for his name's sake," "for my name's sake," or "for your name's sake." "Name's sake" refers to reputation.

We may tell God, "Look how well I've done!" but He may reply, "You should see what you could have done if you'd followed My laws! You settled for this? You call this success?"

> *The success of a product is not good for the product—*
> *it's good for the manufacturer.*

LAWS CREATE RELATIONSHIPS

I love this saying by King Solomon: "If the ax is dull and its edge unsharpened, more strength is needed, but skill will bring success." Here's the application: If you don't know and understand the Creator's laws and principles of success, you'll keep working hard, just as you have to do with a dull ax, but you still won't cut the "tree" down. You won't accomplish what you were born to do. You can work diligently and still not be a success—thus failing to reflect the Manufacturer's reputation.

Life is not just about working hard. It's about working skillfully, working smartly. Does your ax need sharpening? Are you merely working hard, or are you working smartly according to life's laws and principles by putting them to work?

For example, the fact that a car needs to run on fuel (or perhaps a combination of fuel and electricity) is a "law" that is built into the vehicle. So, if you want what the manufacturer promises, then you must follow their principles. First, you must *know* what the principle is—in this case, that the car runs on fuel; second, you must *accept* or *submit to* the need to put fuel in your car; and, third, you must actually *put* fuel into your gas tank. This process of knowing, accepting, and taking action applies to all laws and principles and in many contexts of life.

Laws define the way life works. Of course, you can work contrary to a principle. For example, you can put orange juice instead of gasoline in your car, but if you do, you will cancel the manufacturer's promise. The law says your car needs gasoline, and that means you have to go where you can obtain that fuel: a service station. You must maintain a relationship with service stations as long as you own that car. If, one day, you decide that you're no longer going to put gas in the tank of your car, your car will say, "Then you're not going anywhere." You will shut the car down from its purpose. So laws create relationships. You relate to service stations because you want your car to function.

You may not like the idea that you have to go to a service station to get gasoline for your car, but you will need to do many things you may not like in order to keep benefitting from the car's function.

LAWS REPLACE EXPERIMENTATION

When you know laws and principles and learn to relate to them consistently, you no longer need to experiment with life. So laws replace experimentation. You don't have to guess about what to do if you know the principles. The result, therefore, is that you can live life with fewer mistakes and keep moving in the right direction.

Thus, here is a summary of some of the basic properties of laws for us to keep in mind. We will cover additional properties as we go along.

- *Laws are permanent.* They are time-tested, and they don't change like styles or fads do.
- *Laws are universal.* They work anywhere. For example, the physical law of gravity is present around the world, all the time. It's in effect in England, China, Jamaica, Australia—everywhere. It's a law. My point is that if you learn the keys of the kingdom, which are universal and permanent, you can use them no matter where you live. This means that you don't necessarily need to change your

geographical location to be successful, although there are times when you may need to change your environment or location. But success will come looking for you if you follow the laws. Many people think, "If I can just go and live _______________, I'll make it in life." The real issue is, do you know the laws of success?

- *Laws work regardless of circumstances.* This means that they work when things are going well in your life, your community, or your nation; and they work when there is difficulty or crisis in your life, community, or nation.
- *Laws are not partial—they don't show favoritism.* I hope you understand that laws don't work only for people of a particular race, nationality, or social status. To return to the example of physical laws, gravity pulls on people of all races and nationalities. It doesn't give an exception to anyone. The element of fire will burn in the same way in any country of the world; it doesn't change according to a nation or a people group. Similarly, the laws of life work for all people if the people work the laws.

  Keep yourself from the mindset that someone else is successful because they caught a break or had good luck. You don't know what others might have had to deal with—and are still dealing with. If you learn the laws and principles, focusing on your own purpose—not someone else's—you will find success also.

  And don't be envious of those who learned the laws early in life. You can start applying them today.
- *Laws guarantee results and success.* This means that you can actually steer what happens in your life from now on. If you seem to be failing in life, try to study what laws you may be violating. If you are succeeding in life, study the laws you are following so you can better understand your success and build on it.
- *Laws and principles protect the product from abuse.* God gave us laws to protect us. They protect the "products" He created and the purposes for which He created them. The protection comes in obedience to those laws. For example, when you stop at a red light, you don't need to worry about getting a ticket. The protection is in

obeying the law. Guilt comes when you break a law, because you're no longer protected by that law. Obedience to the laws of creation leads to a successful life.

- *Laws serve the product.* If you want success, it is to your benefit to work with laws and principles because they will serve your purpose in life.
- *Laws simplify product operation.* Once more, laws help eliminate the guesswork on how we are to proceed in life.

I cover a number of the Creator's laws of success in this book, but you can read many more in His Manual. When some people think of God's laws, they think only of the Ten Commandments. Believe me, there are many more laws than that. There's really no end to learning them.

One of the ancient psalmists wrote:

> Your commands are always with me
>   and make me wiser than my enemies.
> I have more insight than all my teachers,
>   for I meditate on your statutes.
> I have more understanding than the elders,
>   for I obey your precepts.[29]

I love laws and principles, and I follow them. People think I'm smart, but I just have a good memory for principles, and I put them into practice.

7

ACTIVATE THE LAWS OF SUCCESS

"The secret of success is constancy to purpose."
—Benjamin Disraeli[30]

When you follow your purpose and obey the related laws, you will attract good things, such as opportunities and other benefits—and people will come seeking you. We will talk more about this in the next section of the book. For example, I received a phone call from someone on the board of the NFL who said, "Look, we are having some problems with NFL players. They're having difficulties." He talked about how their marriages were breaking up, and how they were having issues in other areas. Then he said, "You're the man that we want to come in and talk to the players."

"Me?" I asked.

"Yes," he replied. "We've read some of your material. We want to retain you as a consultant."

Being a consultant for the NFL was not something I pursued, and it would have been unlikely to predict given my geographical location. My home is on an island that is only seven miles wide. I hadn't moved to a major metropolitan area to try to get a better job or to advance my career. Success and influence came looking for me when I wasn't even looking for them. All I was doing was continuing to follow the Creator's laws and principles that I had learned.

ALIGNED WITH PURPOSE

One of the first statements Jesus of Nazareth made about law is this one:

> Do not think that I have come to abolish the Law or the Prophets; I have not come to abolish them but to fulfill them. For truly I tell you, until heaven and earth disappear, not the smallest letter, not the least stroke of a pen, will by any means disappear from the Law until everything is accomplished.[31]

The earth is still here, so the laws still apply.

Jesus said something additional about laws that relates to our success:

> Anyone who sets aside one of the least of these commands and teaches others accordingly will be called least in the kingdom of heaven, but whoever practices and teaches these commands will be called great in the kingdom of heaven.[32]

Jesus indicated that when you learn how important laws are, and when you practice them and teach them to others, you will become great.

God told Moses's successor, Joshua, the same secret to success:

> Be strong and very courageous. Be careful to obey all the law my servant Moses gave you; do not turn from it to the right or to the left, that you may be successful wherever you go. Keep this Book of the Law always on your lips; meditate on it day and night, so that you may be careful to do everything written in it. Then you will be prosperous and successful.[33]

Note once more that God put the responsibility of success on Joshua, not on Himself. God was saying, "If you keep My laws and obey My commands, if you do not turn from them to the right or to the left, if you meditate on them day and night and get them into your circuits, your system, I guarantee that you will make your way prosperous, and you will be successful."

I have underscored that both success and failure are predictable. So, you can actually reverse this statement: "If you do *not* keep this Book of the Law always on your lips, and do *not* meditate on it day and night, and are *not* careful to do everything written in it, then you will be unprosperous and unsuccessful."

Suppose you put a wheat seed on a tile floor and left it there for twenty years. The seed would just sit there, and it would probably disintegrate over time. You might pray for twenty years over that seed on the tile floor, asking God to make it grow. But all your prayers would not bring a wheat plant from that seed. Laws cannot be substituted for by prayer. Likewise, prosperity doesn't come by prayer alone but by keeping laws.

God doesn't answer prayer because we pray loudly or even emotionally. We have to come to Him with His keys. Your emotions don't open doors. You have emotions after the blessing comes. You don't stand by the door and say, "Open." The door will answer, "No. You need a key, and the right key, too. Don't just come here with any key and expect me to open."

God is compassionate and forgiving, and, as I said earlier, He is able to meet all types of needs that we may have; His names tell us that He will supply whatever we might need at a given moment. But here we are talking about how to implement laws and know that we have done our part in the process of success. We cannot ignore His laws even as we look for His help and guidance.

Jesus indicated that when you learn how important laws are, and when you practice them and teach them to others, you will become great.

SHORTCUTS: THE LONGEST WAY TO SUCCESS

The way to a successful life is order, or being aligned with what God has purposed and planned, and order comes from law. Jesus of Nazareth indicated the same thing when He said, "Seek first his [God's] kingdom and his righteousness [or righteous laws], and all these things [everything needed for everyday life] will be given to you as well."[34] By using the word "first," Jesus was indicating priority. He valued the kingdom, the influence of heaven on earth, more than anything else.

Sometimes, people expect God to do magic. These people look for miracles all the time. When certain religious leaders asked Jesus for a miraculous sign, He replied, "A wicked and adulterous generation asks for a sign!"[35] In other words, they were looking for shortcuts.

To take a shortcut means to go against a law or laws. Let me tell you: *The longest way to success is the shortcut.*

In the writings of the New Testament, there are several accounts describing Jesus being tempted by Satan, or the devil. One of the greatest temptations the devil levied on Jesus was this one: he took Him to the highest pinnacle of the temple and said, "If You really are who You say You are—jump! You won't hurt Yourself—God's Word says that He will protect You."[36]

In other words, the devil was telling Him to take a shortcut. "Don't go through all the pain and suffering of the crucifixion. Just get it over with. If You jump now and live, they'll believe in You."

But Jesus answered, "It is also written: 'Do not put the Lord your God to the test.'"[37]

If you cut across somebody's yard instead of going along the main road, you call it a shortcut, don't you? But what are you really doing? Trespassing.

Jesus taught His disciples to pray, "Forgive us our debts,"[38] which is often expressed as, "Forgive us our trespasses." In other words, "God, forgive us for trying to quicken things in life by avoiding the process of following Your laws. Forgive us for trying to use schemes that will get us there faster." This is why people get into problems in business, attempting get-rich-quick schemes. This is also why gambling is destructive—it encourages shortcuts. I guarantee you that a person who has a habit of gambling will always lose money and/or be poor. Even if they win once, they can end up poor. We can't go against laws and not experience the consequences.

Don't take shortcuts to find your own way of doing things. The Creator has established laws in life for everyone to follow for the most successful results.

Everybody else may think you are successful, but have you actually been failing because you haven't been doing what God has planned for your life? We read in the book of Jeremiah, "'I know the plans I have for you,' declares the LORD, 'plans to prosper you and not to harm you, plans to give you hope and a future.'"[39] God has a future, a mark, ahead of you that's supposed to be what you reach. If you don't make it to the future God intended, no matter how many people have celebrated you along the way, you aren't a success because you haven't fulfilled your purpose.

GROWING WITH LAWS AND PRINCIPLES

God tells us, "I will give you the keys, I will give you the principles, the systems, the concepts by which you will have success." My desire is to help you see your purpose and align your life with that purpose so that you can be successful. Here are some ways in which following laws and principles enable us to develop personally, building us up so we can achieve success. Laws and principles give us...

PEACE AND CONFIDENCE

When you know the laws, you can have peace and confidence because you understand the way forward and trust in the process of success, and you don't let naysayers discourage you. I teach the laws and principles of success with full confidence because I have learned them, I have tested them, and I have personally proved them. I can affirm that these laws work.

BOLDNESS

Laws and principles are the enemies of fear. When you know the laws of life, you don't have to be afraid of negative circumstances because you understand that you can respond to them with the appropriate principles. Fear is often evidence of ignorance.

If you know you have half a million dollars in the bank, and everybody around you is panicking because they don't have any money and the economy is unstable, are you going to panic along with them? No. Why not? You can't physically see the money in the bank, but you're going to remain calm because you know that the money is there for you if you need it. Similarly, the resources you need to follow your purpose are found in God's laws—to be put into effect as you need them.

Jesus Christ had confidence and boldness even when facing death. This wasn't simply because He was God. It was because He had knowledge. He said, "My Father told Me that if I lay My life down, I can take it up again."[40] It was information that gave Him confidence and boldness. Knowing laws reduces and cancels fear.

Laws and principles are the enemies of fear.

UNDERSTANDING AND WISDOM

A knowledge of laws and principles is also the source of wisdom. One of my favorite statements in the Bible, which has given me key guidance in my life, is from the book of Proverbs, where Solomon wrote, "The beginning of wisdom is this: Get wisdom. Though it cost all you have, get understanding."[41] I have lived on that truth for decades.

Solomon was talking about laws here. If you understand laws, you become wise. As I mentioned earlier, when we start following the laws of creation, or the laws of life, people will think that we are naturally wise or smart when we're actually just knowledgeable about those laws. They call that wisdom. I am counseling people who are at the head of their government, and they think I'm wise. No, I just know the laws of leadership. I know the laws of communication. I know the laws of social development. I know the laws of family security. So, I just repeat the laws, and people respond to them because the laws make sense.

Wisdom is the application of time-tested laws and principles. Three words we want to keep in mind are *knowledge, understanding,* and *wisdom.* Knowledge is information, and understanding is comprehension, but wisdom is application. You may actually know laws but not apply them. If so, the result will be the same as if you didn't know the laws: you will flounder and fail.

POWER AND STRENGTH

Laws and principles are more important than power because employing them is what leads to power. When a person knows laws, they will find that they have various types of power related to exercising their purpose and gifting. We'll talk more about this in coming chapters.

God told Joshua to "be *strong* and very courageous" by keeping the laws. Your strength is proven by the laws you know and the laws you obey. For example, in the Ten Commandments, why did God say not to kill? Because when you kill, not only do you destroy a life, but you also affect everything connected with that life. Those commandments are divine laws for the protection of all life. If you preserve life, you will make your way prosperous.

There are two more aspects of the laws of life that we must understand in order to activate them: the unique qualities of natural and spiritual laws, and the difference between laws and rules. We'll explore these topics next.

8

NATURAL LAWS AND SPIRITUAL LAWS

"Gravity explains the motions of the planets, but it cannot explain who sets the planets in motion."
—Isaac Newton[42]

As we follow the laws of the Creator while serving our gift, it's important to recognize how natural laws and supernatural laws are both similar to and different from one another. This will keep us from mistaking one for the other and enable us to effectively apply them.

NATURAL LAWS

1. *Natural laws were established by the Creator.* For instance, no human being created the laws of gravity, motion, or thermodynamics. God's wonderful design of the universe created these things.

2. *Natural laws establish natural order.* The word *natural* is derived from the word *nature*. Thus, whatever is built into nature is what we call "natural"—it is generally the way things work in the created world.

3. *Natural laws regulate natural relationships.* We talked about how a tree is connected to the soil in which it is planted. The tree and the soil have a relationship according to natural law. There are many such natural relationships on earth. For example, we human beings don't produce oxygen ourselves, but it's a physical law that we need to breathe oxygen to live. Plants and trees produce oxygen, so we have a relationship with them; we have to protect and nurture trees for our own sake. That's a relationship based on a law.

4. *Natural laws cannot be changed.* They are inherent in the environment of the created world.

5. *Natural laws have built-in ramifications or consequences* depending on how we respond to them. I mentioned earlier how, if a tree were to be uprooted from the soil in which it was planted, we wouldn't have to guess what would happen to it. The judgment from its disconnection to what sustains it is built into the natural law governing it. Similarly, a fish has a relationship with water; it needs to live in water to survive. If a fish were to jump out onto dry land, it would suffer the consequences of that disconnection.

Similarly, if a human being were to try to defy a natural law, such as gravity, by jumping from a great height, they would probably be killed or at least critically injured. Once more, what this tells us is that success—and failure—is predictable.

Let's now look at the nature of spiritual laws.

SPIRITUAL LAWS

1. *Spiritual laws were established by the Creator,* just as natural laws were.

2. *There are spiritual laws that are inherent in the human spirit.* All of us, whether or not we believe in a Creator, generally know when we're doing something we shouldn't do or violating the law. This is because spiritual laws are built into us as human beings. There is a spiritual law within your being called the *conscience.* No one has to tell you when you're committing a wrong or when you need to do the right thing—an internal law tells you that. But you have a choice whether to listen to and follow that law. For example, people can be aware, through their conscience, that they are

consistently doing something that is bad for them, but their habit controls them, and they keep doing it anyway.

3. *Spiritual laws regulate supernatural relationships.* For you to relate to God, you have to obey some spiritual laws. The first of those laws is submission. You have to yield to God. God can't help you if you don't yield to Him. Second, you have to confess to Him that you don't know anything! That's a spiritual law. You can't go to God as if you are the end-all of everything and have no need for Him. This law of submission applies to your body; your mind, or your intelligence; and your spirit.

4. *Spiritual laws are eternal.* They are not limited to the laws of the finite world; they transcend nature.

5. *Spiritual laws have built-in ramifications or consequences.* Like natural laws, spiritual laws have their own inherent results. If we obey these laws, we reap positive consequences. If we disobey them, we reap negative consequences. When our forefather, Adam, decided to act in a way that was contrary to the Creator's law, the Creator didn't punish him with death—death was built into this law: "You are free to eat from any tree in the garden; but you must not eat from the tree of the knowledge of good and evil, for when you eat from it you will certainly die."[43] God didn't say, "On the day that you eat fruit from that tree, I will kill you!" No, the dying was built into the act of violating that spiritual law. God doesn't need to judge us. That's how powerful laws are. Paul of Tarsus expressed it in this way: "The wages of sin is death."[44]

God was saying, "Look, your relationship with Me depends on your obeying this law. I'm not going to kill you, but if you partake of that tree, you are breaking faith with My commandment." It's not the tree itself—it's the fact that God established a law not to eat from it.

So, just like a tree being uprooted from the soil where it is planted, or a fish leaping into an environment without water, when people decided to leave God, they spiritually died, and eventually physically died. The relationship was determined by the laws that were set in place at the beginning of creation. That's why God sent Jesus to earth to restore the connection between human beings and Himself—so we could be given new life and be able to follow His laws of life once more. Here is Paul's statement again with the phrase that follows it: "The wages of sin is death, but the gift of God is eternal life in Christ Jesus our Lord."[45]

No one has to tell you when you're committing a wrong or when you need to do the right thing—an internal law tells you that.

6. *Spiritual laws can overrule natural ones.* There are times when the Creator will act in a way that is contrary to natural laws in order to carry out His purposes on earth. Merriam-Webster online dictionary gives various definitions for *law* that give us insight into this. One definition reads in this way: "a statement of an order or relation of phenomena that so far as is known is invariable under the given conditions."[46] Physical laws have been established for the normal course of life on earth, and they hold true in that context. However, when spiritual laws enter the picture, natural laws are not necessarily "invariable." For example, to allow the Israelites to escape from the pursuing Egyptians, God parted the Red Sea;[47] when this occurred, the waters seemed to function against the law of gravity. In another example, Jesus walked on water, which, for a human being, isn't physically possible from a natural law standpoint.[48] This is where God's supernatural laws override natural laws.

MAXIMUM FULFILLMENT OF PURPOSE AND POTENTIAL

The laws of the Creator are therefore both natural and supernatural, both physical and spiritual, to guarantee the maximum fulfillment of our purpose and potential. In other words, God created all the laws to work in our favor. Once more, the problem many of us have in life is simple: we don't know the laws. So, we come to life experimenting, guessing, hoping things will work out for us.

My purpose and work are to teach, consult, and advise people, and I consider my role to be clear and straightforward: I help people understand laws. It isn't anything mysterious or complex. Every day, I just teach laws.

Laws don't take into account personal opinion. Whenever I give people advice, I focus on laws rather than my opinion. God's laws are not suggestions. They are instructions, and we want to receive His instructions.

As I expressed earlier, a speaker might say things that make people feel good for the moment, but, in the end, did their listeners learn anything that can benefit their lives? Did they learn any laws of personal success? Some people have been listening to the same speakers or influencers for years, but they're still broke, depressed, and frustrated; they still don't know how to succeed. It's not someone's speaking or even preaching that sets you free. It's putting into practice the truth of the laws that sets you free and enables you to succeed.[49]

The concept of need is related to laws. We don't "want" God—we *need* God. That's the reason many people come back to the Creator and His purposes. When we find out who He is, then we want Him because we learn what He is truly like. People think that coming to God is a religious experience. No, it isn't. It's about coming to our senses. Plants need soil. Fish need water. People need the Creator.

Jesus taught that, without God, we can do nothing.[50] Without soil, plants can do nothing. Without water, fish can do nothing. Without God, we can do nothing. This is not a matter of choice; it's a matter of order that is built into the laws of life and creation.

Humans are the only created beings who willfully and intentionally question, challenge, walk away from, and go against spiritual and natural laws. Fish never willingly leave water. Plants never willingly leave the soil. They don't challenge the law. Challenging these laws puts us in a predicament. That's why we are seeing forms of failure all over the world. In every culture, every race, every ethnic group, people are failing by the billions because they either don't know natural and spiritual laws, or they intentionally act in a way that is contrary to them.

Remember that God told Moses's successor, Joshua, "If you obey My laws, you will be successful and prosperous."[51] One Bible version translates the ending phrase as "you will have good success."[52] That expression "good success" reminds us that we can have bad success. A drug dealer may have a lot of money, but he probably can't sleep at night. Why? There may be people who are out to kill him, so he has to stay up all night guarding his money. That is not prosperity. That is torment.

> *It's not someone's speaking or even preaching that sets you free. It's putting into practice the truth of the laws that sets you free and enables you to succeed.*

LAWS GIVE YOU CONTROL OVER LIFE

Jesus made a simple comment that people often don't even think about. First, He said, "A man scatters seed on the ground." Now watch what He said next: "Night and day, whether he sleeps or gets up, the seed sprouts and grows, though he does not know how. All by itself the soil produces grain—first the stalk, then the head, then the full kernel in the head."[53]

Jesus didn't say, "A man scatters seed on the ground. Then he goes to bed, worrying and praying about that seed; he gets up and strives to make that seed grow, saying, 'Seed, germinate! Seed, spring up!'" No, He said, "A man goes out and sows seed in the soil. Then, each night, he sleeps, and each day he gets up and goes about his day, and all the while his seed is growing and developing on its own." In other words, after sowing the seed, the man doesn't think about it anymore. Why? Because he reasons, "I've done what I'm supposed to do. I've obeyed the laws. I can go to sleep at night without worrying about it." He knows the harvest is coming. This is what I meant when I said that laws give us peace and confidence.

This is difficult for many people because they want to help the Creator. They feel like if they aren't doing something, then they aren't doing anything. Jesus says, "No, once you plant, you go to sleep." Why? Because, as I mentioned previously, the laws work automatically once you engage them. Once you obey them, they have their own internal productivity. They begin to produce.

To use another car illustration, if you go to the gas station and fill your car with gasoline, do you then pray for the car to have fuel so it can run?

No. You have obeyed the law that your car functions on gasoline, so now you just start the engine and press the gas pedal to be on your way.

Thus, when you know and obey the laws of life, you control the outcome. I'm not implying that we shouldn't submit our plans to the Creator and talk with Him about our concerns. But I am saying that we shouldn't just hope something works out rather than putting God's laws into practice—laws that He has already established for us to employ for our success.

The Creator has given us an Owner's Manual filled with the laws of life and creation. He gave us these laws so we would know what it means to live according to His nature and ways. Yet God's desire was not to have His laws recorded merely on stone or even paper. God revealed His ultimate plan with these words, which He gave to the prophet Jeremiah: "I will put my law in their minds and write it on their hearts."[54]

9

LAWS VERSUS RULES

"The ultimate measure of a man is not
where he stands in moments of comfort and
convenience but where he stands at times of
challenge and controversy."
—Martin Luther King Jr.[55]

Once we understand the foundations of the Creator's laws and their relationship to success, it's essential to make a distinction between a law and a "rule." We can't afford to confuse one with the other. Knowing the distinction eliminates frustration and confusion. Following the laws of life is the bedrock of success, but following "rules" can actually prevent you from being successful. Many people's lack of success in life is due to the fact that they have been obeying the rules. Anyone who wants to be successful must break some rules!

To contrast the two concepts, let's briefly review the nature of the laws of life before looking at the nature of rules.

THE NATURE OF LIFE'S LAWS

One of the reasons I talked about the qualities of natural laws and spiritual laws is that it helps us to see the differences between laws and rules. We know that laws are the inherent or built-in principles that regulate life and relationships within creation. This means:

- *True laws and principles can never be broken.* We don't "break" laws, even though we often use that terminology to describe going against a law. In other words, when we disobey a law, it doesn't have an effect on the law—the law remains intact. Instead, it has an effect on us and our lives.
- *True laws and principles break those who go against them.* Again, if you were to jump from the top of a ten-story building, you wouldn't violate gravity—gravity would violate you. You wouldn't push yourself down; gravity would pull you down.
- *The Creator does not have to impose judgment when we go against His laws and principles.* Once more, we make this conclusion based on the first two points. It is what I mean by laws having inherent judgment built into them.
- *True laws and principles attract and activate their own rewards when they are put into practice.* This is why I have said that failure or success is not up to God. God has finished establishing natural and spiritual laws. He created everything and put the laws in motion. It is up to us to follow them to be successful.

THE NATURE OF RULES

Now consider the above points in contrast to rules, which we could also refer to as traditions. People sometimes think of laws and rules as the same thing, yet if you're going to be successful, you have to keep the law but violate certain traditions.

When Jesus talked about our becoming great by practicing and teaching the commands of the law, He also said, "For I tell you that unless your righteousness surpasses that of the Pharisees and the teachers of the law, you will certainly not enter the kingdom of heaven."[56] What does it mean to have "righteousness"? It simply means to be aligned with God's laws.

Jesus is talking here about the difference between following tradition and obeying laws. He addressed this issue many times in His ministry. Later on, some religious leaders asked Jesus, "Why do your disciples break the tradition of the elders?"[57]

Whose tradition were they speaking about? That of the elders, not of God. Thus, you must separate what human beings have established from what God has established. Not everything that humans have established is wrong. Some of it has been built upon the laws and principles of success that the Creator has put into place. But I guarantee you with all my strength that following man-made traditions and rules will undermine your purpose and lead to failure.

Jesus responded to the religious leaders in this way: "And why do you break the command of God for the sake of your tradition?"[58] In other words, "Why do you break the laws of God in order to follow your rules?" This difference between laws and rules is vital to remember throughout your life in order to keep fulfilling your purpose and attain success.

Anyone who wants to be successful must break some rules!

RULES CAN BE DANGEROUS

Several other dictionary definitions of *law*[59] give us insights into the difference between laws and rules. Let's take a look at them:

1. "The revelation of the will of God set forth in the Old Testament"; "the first part of the Jewish scriptures: pentateuch, torah." The Pentateuch is the first five books in the Bible: Genesis, Exodus, Leviticus, Numbers, and Deuteronomy. These definitions of *law* would include many of the laws of God. The rules of men that are contrary to the Creator's laws will inevitably make people fail, keeping them from true prosperity and success.

2. "A binding custom or practice of a community: a rule of conduct or action prescribed or formally recognized as binding or enforced by

a controlling authority." People call this "law," but it's actually a rule if it is based only on people's custom or practice and not on the laws of creation.

This kind of "law" can be dangerous. For example, it was originally written into America's constitution that, for the purpose of the census, Black slaves would be counted as only three-fifths of "free Persons." This implied that the other two fifths were what? Animal? That was a law, and people were expected to follow it in their procedures. That law implied that a Black slave could never be treated like a human being who was equal to anyone else, so they could be sold just as animals were sold. The rule supported the institution of slavery, which was already legal and practiced in the country.

Though there were individuals and groups in America who opposed slavery, the majority of the white community in the country consented to the "rule" that Black people were not fully human. It was acceptable to sell them as property and to hold them against their will, to beat them, and to brand them with a hot iron just as people would brand a cow. Again, the whole concept was supported by a rule created by the community, and it was binding and enforceable by a controlling authority. The community made that enforceable. That's how dangerous man-made laws can be. Some human rules are designed to restrict and control other human beings. They are imposed on people to retard their power.

What happened to abolish slavery in America? There were people who rose up and said, "We are against that rule because there's a higher law. There's a divine law that says that all humans are created equal, and that they are all made in God's image." Where did they get that law? From the book of Genesis and other parts of the Bible. The law became more important than the rule, and slavery was eventually abolished. You can see why I don't trust the rules of men.

3. "A command or provision enacted by a legislature." This may be the definition with the most frightening ramifications. People are enacting all kinds of laws today that I call rules because they are based on mere man-made ideas and are contrary to the laws of God.

THE DIFFERENCE BETWEEN LAWS AND RULES

In light of these definitions and the properties of the Creator's laws, we can come to these conclusions:

1. *Laws are more important than rules.* They were established in creation and are unchanging. They supersede rules.

2. *Laws are different from rules.* Laws are permanent, while rules are temporary and formulated on the consensus of members of a community, legislature, or other ruling authority.

3. *Rules are man-made customs and boundaries.* Human beings were designed by God to live according to, and to protect, natural law and divine law. What humanity has essentially attempted to do is to create a third set of laws, one of its own. Many times, these laws go against (or attempt to go against) the first two sets of laws. When people institute such rules, they create limitations for other people.

4. *Laws should never be subject to rules.* Martin Luther King Jr. said these words when he was fighting against the oppression of white domination in America: "There are two types of laws: There are just laws and there are unjust laws. I would be the first to advocate obeying just laws. One has not only a legal but a moral responsibility to obey just laws. Conversely, one has a moral responsibility to disobey unjust laws."[60]

5. *Where there is conflict between a law and a rule, obey the law.* There comes a point when we cannot allow laws to be subject to rules if we are going to fulfill our purpose and be successful. That might even mean going to jail. Martin Luther King Jr. went to prison because he broke a rule. He broke the rule that says people are unequal. Why? Because he, too, found a higher law that says all people are equal. King obeyed the law and violated the rule even though he had to pay a price.

6. *Successful people always break rules for the sake of laws.* I remember when it was said that no man could break the four-minute mile—people thought a human being couldn't run a mile in a faster time than four minutes. This was an unwritten rule, not a natural law. Then, one man named Roger Bannister decided, "I'm going to break that rule." Once he broke it, many others broke it as well. Leaders are always rule-breakers. That's why they're leaders. You can't lead by keeping rules. You lead by keeping laws.

People create various types of rules all the time. Many people once believed that a computer had to be as big as a room because that's what computers were originally like. Then the desktop computer, the handheld computer, the wrist computer, and the eyeglasses computer were invented. Why? People keep breaking the rules made by men. If you want to be successful, find a rule to break. Some of these rules are technological and some are social and cultural. For example, some people believe that a person of a particular background, education, or culture can't do or achieve certain things. They have rules for who is able (or allowed) to be successful in various aspects of life. Somebody is going to come along and break those rules because they are man-made.

7. *Never be afraid to break the rules for the sake of the law of God in creation.* I believe rules by men were made to be broken. Only those who break them make history.

Suppose you have a *job* in a hotel, but the God-given dream within you is to *own* a hotel. You may think, or you may hear someone say, "You could never own a hotel; you come from a poor family." Who is telling you that you can't do it? That's the question. Like the religious leaders in Jesus's day, are they making the rules of men more important than the laws of God? You have to settle the issue of which you are going to follow: rules or laws. Sometimes we make up rules for ourselves that have no basis in the laws of life. Remember, exercising laws leads to confidence and boldness, not fear.

The following are several statements by Jesus of Nazareth that we can apply to obeying laws and breaking rules:

"Everything is possible for one who believes."[61] To do the "impossible," we must believe in God's laws over man's rules. Success begins by ignoring and violating human rules and limitations.

"Therefore I tell you, whatever you ask for in prayer, believe that you have received it, and it will be yours. And when you stand praying, if you hold anything against anyone, forgive them, so that your Father in heaven may forgive you your sins."[62] When we are following the Creator's laws for life and relationships, we can be assured that He will support us in exercising the gift He has placed within us.

"The knowledge of the secrets of the kingdom of heaven has been given to you, but not to them."[63] Others have their rules, but you have the laws of the kingdom. Remember that Jesus also said, "I will give you the keys of the kingdom of heaven, and whatever you bind [lock up] on earth will be bound [locked up] in heaven, and whatever you loose [unlock] on earth will be loosed [unlocked] in heaven."[64] Every time you come across a man-made lock, unlock it. You have the keys, so keep unlocking.

Every time you come across a man-made lock, unlock it. You have the keys, so keep unlocking.

Successful people know laws that unlock the locks of men. People will try to lock you up and lock you down. They will tell you that you can't do what you're meant to do. They might say, "You could never be a clothes designer. There's too much competition." God says, "No, I have given you the vision and the gifts to be a clothes designer, and I will show you how to make it happen."

I was never supposed to be able to do what I'm doing. I violated man-made rules for what I could accomplish. So, I want to encourage you: break some rules!

PART THREE

INNOVATION, EXCELLENCE, AND PROSPERITY

10

PURPOSE AND PLANS

"Many are the plans in a person's heart, but it is the LORD's purpose that prevails."
—King Solomon[65]

I know firsthand the principle that your purpose and gift will preserve you. I mentioned that I was born into a poor family. I have written elsewhere about what it was like for me growing up, so you may be familiar with my story. I was one of eleven children, and I lived in a wooden two-bedroom house in Bain Town, the poorest village on the island of New Providence in the Bahamas. My father and mother slept in one bedroom, which was separated from the other bedroom by a partition, and my seven sisters slept in beds in the second room, while my three brothers and I slept there on the wood floor. I remember feeling the rats run over my body during the night. I would also have blood all over my body every morning because the mosquitoes would eat me alive in the heat.

When it rained, the water would drip down on me. I'd get buckets and put them under the spots where the leaks were, and I would have to sleep between the buckets. I owned one pair of shoes for the whole year, and when the shoes developed holes in the bottoms, I would put cardboard in the soles. I would also go to school barefoot. I know what it is like to eat corned beef out of a can for Sunday dinner and to have a chicken neck only on special occasions. So, poverty is something with which I am familiar. I also grew up knowing about religion—and I learned that religion doesn't help. That's why I talk about the kingdom. The kingdom of God is not the same thing as religion.

As I wrote earlier, learning about the kingdom taught me my purpose. By pursuing that purpose and following the laws of life, I was able to attend a university even though I had no money. Provision became available for me. My parents never paid a cent for the education I received. In fact, I used to send money home to my parents when I was in college. If you haven't yet discovered your purpose, you must find it. No one can keep someone down who knows their purpose. If you're not currently living according to your purpose, I believe you're reading this book so that you can start over.

PRINCIPLES OF PURPOSE

King Solomon wrote, "Many are the plans in a person's heart, but it is the LORD's purpose that prevails." In another Bible translation, this statement ends with the phrase "the LORD's counsel—that will stand."[66] You have all these plans for your life—what you want to do, where you want to go, whom you want to marry, what you want to build, what kind of business you want to open, and so forth. But God says, "Look, I have a purpose for your life that will make you the most fulfilled and successful." We can learn three things from Solomon's statement:

1. *Purpose precedes plans.* Before you were even alive to start making plans, God had a purpose in mind for your life.

2. *Purpose is more important than plans.* Some of your current plans might already align with God's purpose, but you must make a point of evaluating them in light of the purpose and gifting He has given you, and of altering them if needed.

3. *Purpose is more powerful than plans.* Why is this the case? God says, "My purpose will prevail over your plans."

Remember that God doesn't start anything until He's "finished" it, so you're already finished. You have big dreams within you because you're seeing your end. The Scriptures say that Jesus endured the cross—with its accompanying criticism, maligning, and shame—and fulfilled His purpose because He saw His end: "the joy that was set before Him."[67] He saw Himself sitting on the throne, reigning. I wonder what you see. Stop being afraid of it. And stop being afraid of yourself. Don't settle for what you currently have. Go back to your dream—the one that won't quit, the one that keeps "prevailing"—and the one that you're smothering with your busyness. As I wrote in chapter 2, become like a child again and allow yourself to dream once more.

When I was forty years old, I told my father, "I want to travel around the world, and I want to advise governments." My father asked, "Do you believe this is possible, son?" I said, "Yes." He replied, "Then I don't know how, but you must believe it." My father shared the perspective of Jacob, the father of Joseph, whose story is found in the Bible.

As a seventeen-year-old, Joseph had two dreams in which he saw his family members—including his father, mother, and eleven brothers—bowing down to him. At that time, Joseph was one of the youngest in his family, just a dirty shepherd boy tending smelly sheep. But through his dreams, he saw his God-given purpose, or "end." He didn't know any of the details of that purpose, and those details would take years to unfold, but the dreams depicted his eventual position as a ruler in Egypt—second only to the pharaoh himself. When Joseph told his father and his brothers about the dreams, his brothers were jealous, and his father rebuked him for implying that he would be above his parents and older brothers. However, the record also says, "But his father kept the matter in mind."[68] Jacob didn't dismiss the matter because he had personal experience with dreams related to the purposes of God. Good parents don't kill their children's dreams—they feed those dreams.

Don't settle for what you currently have.
Go back to your dream—the one that won't quit,
the one that keeps "prevailing."

IS THIS WHAT YOU SAW?

Let me ask you again to take an honest look at where you are at this stage in your life. I imagine that your dream is not what you are doing right now. Your current job isn't what you saw inside you—or it is not all that you saw. Am I correct? If where you are now is not what you saw, then where you are now is only for a limited time. Wherever you are, continue to do your job with excellence, but tell yourself, "This job is only temporary." In this section of the book, we will cover a number of principles of success for work and jobs.

The temporary status of where you currently are extends to other areas of your life as well. Is the house you're living in the one God showed you? Is the car you're driving the one you saw? If what you see is not what you saw, then what you see is transitory. I want you to sit in your house and say, "This house is only temporary." Then I want you to sit in your car and say, "This is my temporary transportation."

Even if you feel that you are doing well financially or professionally, do you sense that there is still something missing or that what you are doing is incomplete? Is this what you saw when you were growing up? When you were fifteen or twenty, what did you dream? (If that is your age right now, what do you see?) Don't stay parked where you are. Get back to your dreams. God is telling you that you can start again—right now.

Maybe you dreamed of traveling the world or of running a business that helps other people in some way. Note that God is only obligated to finance His own programs. If you pursue your God-given dream, the rest—including the finances—will follow.

Some people think of me as a pastor because of the church I founded. That was a stage of my life, and pastoring is a vital role, but it is only a portion of my dreams. It may be the full dream that God has given others, but I have many more aspects to my dreams. I am involved in developing followers into leaders and in consulting. So, I put plans into place for others to take over my pastoral duties. We need to be able to let go of any place that is temporary in our life. We need to keep developing ourselves. Make plans for your replacement so you can go on to the next phase of your life. You're bigger than who you are right now.

Peter thought his life work was to catch fish, but Jesus of Nazareth came along and said to him, "Follow Me, and I will make you a fisher of men."[69] The depth and scope of Peter's purpose was much larger than his role as a fisherman. He became one of Jesus's closest disciples and a great leader in God's kingdom.

Think about how King David got his start. God told the prophet Samuel to go to the home of Jesse in Bethlehem because a king lived there. Samuel was instructed to anoint this individual. So Samuel went to Jesse and said, "The Lord says there's a king in this house—the next king of Israel." I wonder who might be reading this book. Perhaps, inside you, there is a city councilperson, the head of a board of education, or a mayor. Right now, you're working a job doing something else, but there's a king in the house.

Jesse told Samuel, "I have twelve sons." So Samuel said, "Bring them all out." Let's imagine the scene. The first one who comes out is a tall, commanding-looking young man. But Samuel says, "No, that's not him." The second son is strikingly handsome, but Samuel says, "No, that's not the one." The third is well-educated. No. The fourth is muscular. No. Everybody comes out looking good, but being the king wasn't their purpose. After Jesse presents son number eleven, he says, "Well, that's it. Everybody's accounted for." The prophet says, "None of them is the king, but the Lord says there is a king in this house somewhere."

Jesse replies, "I don't have any more sons." Then he suddenly says, "Wait, I have a youngest son, but it can't be him because he's the dirtiest one, the smelliest one, the one out in the wilderness with the sheep." The prophet says, "Go get him and bring him here."

David, the young son who is out with the sheep, is called; as soon as Samuel sees him, the prophet begins to reach toward the oil. He says, "Here comes the king."[70]

The king of Israel was trapped in a shepherd boy. Are you the forgotten one in your family? No one knows your greatness. You may be trapped in the wilderness with the sheep, but I have come to pour oil on your head and tell people that they don't know who you really are. They thought you were the least in your family and would never amount to anything, that you'd get a job and die paying a mortgage. God says nothing like it. You're a business owner, a writer, an artist, a governmental official, a scientist, a teacher, the leader of a nonprofit organization. There's a king sitting in your chair.

The ancient Scriptures tell the story of Abraham, who didn't start fulfilling his purpose until he was seventy-five years old—so there's hope for you![71]

You can tell the Creator that you want to be what He wants you to be. You can ask Him to help you discover who you really are and reconnect with yourself. Don't try to be like someone else. Be yourself, with no more imitation. Nobody knows who you are except the Manufacturer. Again, while you can seek wise counsel from other people, don't just accept others' opinions of you. Be delivered from historical and societal labeling. Meet yourself again. Be childlike. Believe what God showed you so you can fulfill your purpose.

11

ARE YOU EMPLOYED OR DEPLOYED?

"Don't be afraid to give up the good to go for the great."
—John D. Rockefeller[72]

To pursue your purpose and be successful, you must understand that there's a big difference between your job and your work. Never mistake one for the other.

- Your job is your skill. Your work is your gift.
- Your job is what people pay you to do. Your work is what you were born to do.
- Your job is your career. Your work is your life assignment.
- Your job gives you benefits. Your work gives you fulfillment.
- Your job gives you a salary. Your work gives you prosperity.

OUR ECONOMIC PSYCHOLOGY

For many people, especially when there is an economic downturn, a fear of losing their job is one of their greatest concerns. I want to talk about this fear because I believe that our concept of a job is where the problem lies. Suppose you were laid off from your job or were given fewer work hours. If you have placed your hope in your job, then you will feel like your future is being attacked, and that your means of living is being threatened because you are in danger of losing your car and your home. *But no job, in itself, has a future in it. Instead, the future is in the one who holds the job.*

Our problem is that our culture has not trained us to find our gift. It has trained us to find a job. It's as if we believe we were born to be employed. Our economic psychology has made us dependent on the idea of having a job. That has become our curse because a job is really an opportunity someone else offers you. And if somebody offers you an opportunity, they can always take it back. If you build your life on someone else's offer, you are as safe as how they feel at the time, and they can change the way they feel at any point and withdraw that offer.

Don't ever allow an organization or a job to be your hope. For example, we are told, "Go learn a skill and apply for a position." The issue is, a skill is dispensable. That skill might become obsolete, or someone else who has the same skill might be hired for the position instead of us. Or, if you were the most recent employee to be hired, you may be the first to be let go if there are layoffs. Even if you have been at a company for a number of years, it is still the case that every job is temporary. No matter how much your company may praise and love you, you still need to think beyond your position because, if money becomes tight for that business or you get to a certain age, they may tell you goodbye.

This is why it is essential to ask, "What is my gift?" and really study that question. Because, when you discover your true work, you're not afraid to lose your job—you know there's life after it. You may be laid off or fired from a job, but you can never be laid off or fired from your work. Your job might be taken away from you, but no one can ever take your work away from you. If your company threatens to fire you, you can say, "It's okay." They can take away your ability to perform a certain skill, but they can't take away your gift. They can take away your activity, but they can't take away your ability.

If you took a fish out of a stream and put it in a pond, have you taken away its ability to swim? No, the gift went with the fish, even though you "fired" it from the stream. As we talked about in chapter 3, your gift is more important than your skill. Remember, when you leave a job, your gift goes with you! While your skills may be dispensable, your gift is permanent. So, if you are ever laid off or fired, remember that you carry your gift with you, and, wherever you land, keep on swimming. Your employer didn't take your gift away from you—just the location in which you were using that gift.

Your job might be taken away from you,
but no one can ever take your work away from you.

EMPLOYMENT VERSUS DEPLOYMENT

Thus, I want us to change our thinking about our goal in life: we must think beyond a job. We must change our perspective about it and not let fear control us—we need to become free from the "spirit of jobs" so we can ignite the "spirit of work."

Employment means somebody else controls your life.

Deployment means you release what's inside you.

Deployment activates your gift and energizes your life. Always keep in mind that prosperity is not in your job; it is in your work—your gift, your assignment, what you were born to do. This is how you should think: "I was not born to be *employed*—I was born to be *deployed*."

Employment is the opportunity to serve your gift corporately, or in the context of a group, within a certain structure and oversight. But *deployment*—actively living out your purpose—is discovering your gift and serving that gift to the world and to your generation. Serving our gift to the world is also ultimately accomplished in conjunction with other people. Yet when we deploy ourselves, it is because we have found something that is so sweet to do that we initiate our own activity, and others are drawn to it.

For those who are employed, their value is determined by the one who employs them. But those who deploy themselves determine their own value. In this context, by "value," I don't mean their intrinsic value, which they always have as human beings made in the Creator's image and likeness. Instead, I mean the way in which they are viewed and compensated. A salary is really someone else's opinion of how much you are worth. When you deploy yourself, you can establish your own worth. And those who deploy themselves often employ other people. They always benefit others in some way. If you're tired of being merely employed, focus on being deployed.

WHEN YOUR JOB DOESN'T MATCH YOUR WORK

When people's jobs don't match their true work, and when they don't understand their purpose in life, it causes them all kinds of problems, including unhappiness, dissatisfaction, boredom, and bitterness.

Somebody who is in a place where they're not supposed to be is never comfortable. They can even feel tormented there because they're not built for it. One report said that less than one-third of workers in the United States are engaged in their jobs. "Engaged" is defined as "those who are involved in, enthusiastic about and committed to their work and workplace."[73] It seems that two-thirds of the workers covered in this study may be in a job where they can't become who they really are. It's not what they were born to do. Their true gifts aren't being deployed. They are living outside their purpose.

Such people's jobs are essentially suffocating their real gift. These individuals are restricted by what the job tells them they can and can't do. They're always looking for the workday to end because they feel like a bird trapped in a cage for eight hours.

You, too, may be going to a place or working a job from home every day that doesn't allow you to become who you are. The "cage" you are in confines you. A cage allows a bird to fly only within certain limitations. You're still a bird, and you still have the ability to fly high in the sky for miles on end, but you're in a cage. Your ability hasn't left. It's the restrictions that are holding you back. You are told, "This is as far as you can go." You could be trapped in this way for years. If this is your situation, you might always feel irritated or discouraged because you are continually in a place you don't want to be.

Many people who are unhappy at work spend years being merely employed while disturbing everybody else around them with their complaints, saying things like the following: "I don't know why I come here; this is a lousy job." "Management doesn't know what I'm worth." "They don't understand me." "I hate this place." "I'm supposed to get a promotion and a raise. Why is that not happening?" "I'm tired of being here; I want to go home." For ten years, they've been complaining about their job, but still they won't leave.

People's complaints may come from the fact that, because their gift is not being activated, there's no excitement or energy in their lives, and they feel frustrated and angry. In contrast, it's a pleasure to be around someone who is meant to be sitting next to you in your workplace. They are happy and excited to be there, and they help to create a positive environment. When your job is in a place where you feel your creative and/or analytical juices flowing, and where you can release all the desires and gifts within you so that you are deploying your gift, then you can't wait to get there. As a matter of fact, it can be depressing when you reach the end of the day because you don't want to leave! A person who is functioning in their gift wants the days to be longer because they desire to keep doing what they're doing.

If your job is wearing you out, if it isn't the work that you envisioned, and if you keep watching the clock, waiting for the day to be over, then these are strong signs that you are not yet in your true work. You are employed and not deployed. The same may be true if you have experienced a certain degree of success in your place of employment, and you enjoy your job for the most part, but you feel you have reached a plateau, finding yourself restless or bored at times, sensing that there is more within you that is untapped.

This may be why, at the end of the workday, you get in your car and dash home. You feel so free that you call it "being off." Perhaps you should call it "being released." Then what do you do? Go straight to the couch and turn on the TV? Let that practice end. No more spending hours in front of the TV. You have to activate your gift. You're going to tap into your hidden seed, your treasure. When you're deployed, you serve your natural gift to the world, and the world pays you for being yourself. Can you imagine being paid for something you like to do?

Once more, I challenge you to think about where you are in your life, and at your present age—whether you are young, middle-aged, or older. Think about your current situation in relation to what you are discovering in this book. Ask yourself, "What's happening to my life? How many more years might I have left to fulfill my purpose?"

Perhaps you are divorced or widowed, and your life is at a point where you are saying, "What am I supposed to do now?" God says, "I'm going to tell you: find your gift and serve it." I want to reaffirm to you that God created you with a purpose and a seed to fulfill that purpose—and these are the keys to your prosperity, no matter what the circumstances or the stage of your life may be.

WORK IS NOT A CURSE

Many people have difficulty understanding their purpose because they consider work itself to be a burden or a curse. This perspective can come from a misunderstanding of the biblical record. When human beings decided to act in a way that was contrary to the Creator's law, they had to leave the garden, and work became more difficult for them.[74] But work itself is not a punishment from God. Work was established at the *beginning* of creation, before human beings went against God's law. The first book of Moses tells us that, after God created Adam, the first thing He instructed him to do was to work: "The LORD God took the man and put him in the Garden of Eden to work it and take care of it."[75] The Hebrew word for "work" here is *ergon,* which can mean "to cause to exist, produce."[76] Some Bible versions translate *ergon* as "cultivate" and "tend." God instructed us to work because we were created to produce. That has not changed.

So, work is an established law in creation—the law of work. Whatever stops you from working is violating this law. If you want to get something for free or without making an effort, you're violating this law. King David said, "I have never seen the righteous forsaken or their children begging bread."[77] We talked earlier about what it means to be "righteous." It means living in alignment with the laws God has established. It means staying in step with the nature, priorities, and lifestyle of the kingdom. If you stay in line with the laws of creation, you won't be a beggar.

> *Work was established at the beginning of creation, before human beings went against God's law. God instructed us to work because we were created to produce.*

BECOMING RATHER THAN DOING

Jesus of Nazareth said, "My food...is to do the will of him who sent me and to finish his work."[78] His "food"—the sustenance of His being—was to do the will of His Father. That's a vital statement. His work was to do what? The will. What does "the will" refer to? The intent of the Manufacturer who sent Him. We see again that to work is to become what you were born to be.

Thus, success does not come by *doing* something but by *becoming* something. That's why it's tough for people who decide that they want to become who they are and grow the seed inside them. The traditional world has no room for them; it wants them to work for somebody else. But the world will have to *make room* for them.

The secret to success in my life is that I have become who God created me to be. You have to become yourself. Again, the future of your life is in your seed, or your gift. When you deploy yourself, you create your own environment and your own resources. You create your own revenue. And, once more, it starts with a change in thinking. You must understand that you're not a victim of your circumstances or the economic conditions of the day. Pay more attention to the Creator's laws and principles than you do to news reports about the economy.

Some people have multiple gifts, and that can make the process of finding their true work more difficult for them. The answer to this is to decide which gift you're going to focus on. You have to choose one and concentrate on it. You don't want to be a jack-of-all-trades and master of none. You will be paid for what you master. Most people aren't looking for a generalist.

You have something no one else is able to offer. It's going to be birthed right where you are. People might not understand you or your gift at first, but hold on to your dream. What you want to do is to be in a place where you can become who you really are and manifest your work. That's the goal. And your work can actually *become* your job if you are doing what you were born to do.

WHAT ABOUT RETIREMENT?

For many people, the minute they hit age sixty-five, the company they work for is already starting to consider them gone. Often, the longer you've been with a company, the more expensive you are to them because your salary is higher than others'. They are looking for young people coming out of college whom they can hire for less money. If this is your situation, it's time to wake up and think beyond your job. The solution to your future success at any age is not in your job—it's in what you're thinking about beyond the job.

But many people in their fifties and sixties are already thinking about retiring. No matter what age you are, it's important to gain a new perspective about retirement. To me, the "retirement mentality" in our society is dangerous. In our great-grandparents' day, when someone retired at age sixty-five, they often lived only a few more years. Today, because of the increase in life expectancy, people might live to be eighty or eighty-five on average. If you retire at age sixty or sixty-five, you have twenty to twenty-five years left. What are you going to do for another quarter of your life? You need to think in terms that are higher than retirement. If you are young, you have an opportunity to grasp this concept early and avoid mistakes that people older than you have made along the way in regard to their jobs and attitude toward retirement.

The idea of retirement is not in the Bible. It's a cultural concept. We weren't created to stop working. We are never supposed to "retire"; we are simply supposed to finish our work before we leave this earth. Please remember how we are defining *work*: becoming what we were born to be. If you stop becoming, you stop existing. Paul of Tarsus didn't retire before he died. But he did say, "I have fought the good fight, I have finished the race, I have kept the faith."[79] Jesus Christ didn't retire before He left this earth. But He did say, "It is finished."[80] We are to leave only after we finish something.

You might retire from your job, but you can't retire from your gift or your work. I've never seen a fish that says, "I'm tired of swimming. I retire. I'm not swimming any longer." I've never seen a bird that says, "I decided to retire from flying and just sit in my nest." I've never seen a seed that says, "I've retired from bringing forth a plant."

Some of the most miserable people in the world are individuals who are retired. If you are frustrated in life, maybe it's because you haven't been becoming yourself lately. Often, people who live long lives are those who have found something they love to do throughout their life. They have found something that they can't wait to do when they get up in the morning. In fact, functioning in your gift is good for your health. If you have a positive attitude, your immune system can actually find strength from this, which can potentially protect you from getting sick.

Perhaps you have been retired for five years and are beginning to scratch your head, saying, "Why did I retire?" I want to assure you that there's life after retirement, and you still have a future.

> *We are never supposed to "retire"; we are simply supposed to finish our work before we leave this earth.*

IN—BUT NOT OF

Jesus said that we are to be in the world but not of the world.[81] In other words, you can live within the system, but don't allow the system to make you like a caged bird. You are not to be controlled by societal, cultural, or governmental systems. Ask God to show you the difference between your job and your work. I believe something good is going to happen to you when you discover your true work.

Our goal in life is therefore not to be *employed* but to be *deployed*. That's the secret to success. Employment can prepare you for deployment, but deployment activates your gifts. It's the juice that makes you get up in the morning. It energizes your life.

In the next chapter, I'll give you some recommendations for what to do when your job doesn't match your gifting, and how you can transition from your job to your work.

12

TRANSITIONING FROM YOUR JOB TO YOUR WORK

"Far and away the best prize that life offers is the chance to work hard at work worth doing."
—Theodore Roosevelt[82]

We often need to start out being employed at a job as we discover and deploy our true work. You don't have to leave your job right away. I want to show you how to make the most of where you are right now.

Jesus of Nazareth started out having a job. He was carpenter, following in the profession of His earthy father, Joseph.[83] But His work was to redeem the human race—teaching us God the Father's laws and principles and restoring us to a relationship with Him. When Jesus was just twelve years old, He said, "I must be about My Father's business."[84] He already knew what He was meant to do. Jesus also made statements such as these: "I work the works of Him who sent Me. My Father works; therefore I work. I came to complete the work My Father gave Me to do."[85] Jesus was talking about His work, not His job. His work was to fulfill the purpose of the heavenly Father. Have you found your work yet?

PREPARING FOR DEPLOYMENT

Although our goal is deployment, employment can *prepare* us for deployment. As I wrote earlier, when you go to your job, I want you to remember, "This is temporary. I am going to use this opportunity to deploy myself." Stay in your job as you develop your gift. (Remember, you might even find your work in your job. Some people have found it there. For example, someone who was born to sing and who loves singing with a musical group in which they are paid to sing is not going to a job every day but is going to their work.)

My advice is this: while you are at your job, learn as much as you can because, in my view, jobs are opportunities where you are paid to learn. Also, don't necessarily start out by trying to get a job that will only suit what you really like to do. And don't go for a job merely with the motivation of money. Instead, get a job that's available. Many people today don't want a job because they are waiting for one with the "right" salary. It isn't money that makes a job important. What makes a job significant is that you will be paid as you learn some new skills, have some new experiences, and meet some new people.

Sometimes you may be in a job not primarily for the purpose of being able to earn money but for gaining relationships. There are people with whom I used to work years ago, and my relationships with them have lasted, even though we've since gone our separate ways in terms of our work. These relationships have helped me in my life. For example, I used to have a job in a warehouse. One of my former coworkers at that job is now the manager of a bank, and that relationship has opened doors for me. Nurture relationships with the people around you—not for the purpose of "What can I get out of this person?" but for the enrichment of the relationships, which may bear mutual fruit and lead to open doors for you in the future.

Additionally, during difficult times or crisis periods, which we will talk about in more detail in a coming chapter, you may have to take a job just so that you can survive. That is not a season to hold on to your pride, pretending that everything thing is all right and not doing anything about your financial situation to the point that your children go hungry. There are times when you have to get a job until you can get your work back.

Those who know their purpose and understand the success within them will work at any job until it's time for their purpose to manifest. Remember that your job doesn't define you. You are bigger than the job you hold. Therefore, enjoy it for now. Why? You are just passing through that place. It's not your destiny. It's a temporary location for you to learn certain skills and perspectives, and you are paid to learn these things while you're on your way to greatness. This is why you should never despise a job, even as you realize it is temporary.

Learn all you can on your job. Perform that job well but don't depend on it. Begin to ignite your gift and create your work as you execute your job. Inside you is the wealthiest place in the world. As we've talked about, your gift is a seed that is currently ungerminated and unreleased but is full of potential.

> *What makes a job significant is that you will be paid as you learn some new skills, have some new experiences, and meet some new people.*

BECOMING "INDISPENSABLE" AT YOUR JOB

While you are at employed at your job, although you can't fully depend on your position in terms of your financial security, you can actually make yourself so valuable to your company that you're the last one they will want to let go if there's an economic crunch. You can make yourself "indispensable" by enhancing the value you bring to your position.

How do you make yourself valuable as an employee? By refining your gift as you do your job and applying that gift in as many beneficial ways as possible while maintaining a positive attitude. Make yourself so important to the company by investing in your own gift that they won't want you to leave. As far back as I can remember, in every job I had, my employer always wanted me to stay. The last job I resigned from was a position in the government. I resigned five times. Why? They kept refusing to accept my resignation, saying, "We don't want you to leave the system because you work effectively." You should read the book of Daniel in the Bible sometime. Daniel made himself so valuable that the king said he was an excellent worker, and no one could get rid of him.

If people in your company can't wait for you to leave, then you're not an asset and a help to them but a liability and a hindrance. You've made yourself a problem and a nuisance rather than a solution. When a downsizing takes place at a company due to a shortage in the cash flow, often, the first one to be let go is the one who causes all the problems. Their employer is almost happy that there is a fiscal shortfall because they can finally have an excuse to get rid of that person. They know that, in the future, if they need to, they can hire someone else with the same skills and a better attitude.

As a matter of fact, the key to becoming prosperous is to *solve* problems. You are retained for the problems you solve. You are let go for the problems you create. When people ask me how I am doing, my answer is, "I'm a solution, not a problem."

Tell yourself, "I solve problems. That's why I'm valuable." You have to be able to find problems to solve and then solve them. If you are looking for a job or want to improve your position at your company, look for a problem to solve. When you look for a problem and then solve that issue, you may be paid for it. If you make yourself indispensable to people by serving your gift with quality and becoming more and more valuable to them, they won't want to let you go. Use every job you have to refine your work.

DEVELOPING YOUR WORK

How do you go about developing your true work at the same time you're employed at your job? Cultivate the mindset of a producer and make valuable use of the time that is yours.

BECOME A PRODUCER

The most important statement I ever read in the Bible for setting me free from the idea of needing a job or of merely seeking employment is this one from wise King Solomon in Ecclesiastes 11: "Ship your grain across the sea; after many days you may receive a return."[86] Solomon was discussing business. The phrase "ship your grain across the sea" refers to becoming an exporter, while the phrase "receive a return" refers to dividends. He is talking about getting a return on our investment. We're supposed to be producers and export what we produce. Many people just consume rather than produce. Producers are thinkers, while consumers are hoarders. We need to think about ideas and inventions and stir them up inside us.

Solomon also said, "Invest in seven ventures, yes, in eight; you do not know what disaster may come upon the land."[87] This is the same as saying, "Don't put all your eggs in one basket." We'll talk more about this idea in the next chapter when we discuss how to be successful in our domain. But here is a preview: suppose someone is a barber who only cuts hair. They should actually go beyond cutting hair itself, in case their main business slows down for a time or they somehow become unable to use their skill. For instance, they might sell a line of hair products and other items that they have researched and found to be of good quality and for which there is a strong demand. If someone is a carpenter, they might diversify into supplying wood to builders or importing furniture. Such individuals would still be functioning within their gifts—styling, maintaining, and improving hair, and working with wood to create beautiful and functional items—while expanding the breadth and reach of the services and products they offer. These are just some simple examples to show you the possibilities of diversifying.

Solomon continued, "Whoever watches the wind will not plant; whoever looks at the clouds will not reap."[88] The phrase "whoever watches the wind" refers to people who are waiting for ideal conditions or for luck. They hesitate to go out and work—and this means they won't ever reap. There may never be "ideal conditions," so we need to actively plant if we want to reap.

We need to think about ideas and inventions and stir them up inside us.

"SUCCESS AFTER 5:00"

Solomon went on to say this:

> As you do not know the path of the wind, or how the body is formed in a mother's womb, so you cannot understand the work of God, the Maker of all things. Sow your seed in the morning, and at evening let your hands not be idle, for you do not know which will succeed, whether this or that, or whether both will do equally well.[89]

Sow your seed when? In the morning. What should you do in the evening? Not let your hands be idle. This is among the best advice I have ever heard. We need to pay attention to these wise words. Here's the application: "Go to work in the morning, and when you get off from your job, keep working." Work on your skill during the day, and work on your gift afterward.

When you have a job, the only life you "own" is after 5:00 p.m. During the day while you are doing your job, you can't read books to expand your knowledge in relation to your gift, and you can't experiment with ideas. The hours between 8:00 a.m. and 5:00 p.m.—or whatever specific hours you work—belong to someone else's gift. Your company tells you when to come, where to go, what to do, what time to have lunch, when the workday ends, and so on, and therefore they control your entire day. This means that, although you should seek to apply your gift to your job, making yourself indispensable, you mainly grow in your gift on your own time. After hours, and when the weekend comes, that time fully belongs to your gift. So, give your employer your *skill* at 8:00 a.m., and release your *gift* at 5:00 p.m. This is a great key to success and prosperity.

I want to encourage you that what you're doing now isn't anything compared to what you could be doing! There's life after your job. I call it "Success after 5:00," or "Success after sunset." Work persistently on developing your gift. My organization was built after 5:00 p.m. I had a day job at that time, and so did those who helped me to create the organization. We used to meet after finishing our jobs for the day, and we would work until two in the morning to establish it.

Many successful people began igniting their gift while others were sleeping. I probably do more work while other people are sleeping than they do when they are awake! Of course, we all need a certain amount of rest, and people have different types of responsibilities to fulfill, but note what Solomon said in a proverb about "loving" sleep: "Do not love sleep or you will grow poor; stay awake and you will have food to spare."[90] Our culture says, "Go home and rest after work; you deserve it. Relax and watch TV." The Manufacturer's Manual says, "Let your hands not be idle." Anyone who is a successful businessperson will tell you the same thing that the Manual does. Many people think they want to go into business, but they don't know the commitment it takes; idleness is not part of it. Those who are successful make that commitment because they have found something more important than a job.

Note the second part of this statement from Solomon from the earlier passage in Ecclesiastes: "Sow your seed in the morning, and at evening let your hands not be idle, *for you do not know which will succeed, whether this or that, or whether both will do equally well.*" You can have a job after your job or on the weekend, and both together can bring in a good sum. And you can actually work yourself out of a job. Your work can become so powerful that you don't need your job any longer.

Another wise saying of Solomon is this one: "A man's gift makes room for him, and brings him before great men."[91] It doesn't say, "A man's education makes room for him." You may have a PhD and still be broke, because a PhD alone doesn't make you wealthy. Some people with PhDs have been hired by those who dropped out of school. Why? Because the person who doesn't have a PhD got an idea, and when they acted on that idea, it brought them prosperity. I am certainly a proponent of education, but it's not your education that brings you before great men—it's your gift.

Give your employer your skill at 8:00 a.m., and release your gift at 5:00 p.m. This is a great key to success and prosperity.

That's why just attending a university doesn't make you successful. You don't go to a school to get your gift. Education can help to *refine* your gift, but it can't *give* it to you. Your gift was placed within you by the Manufacturer. So, allow your seed-gift to germinate.

BE READY FOR THE TESTING!

As you enter into your true work, keep in mind that all gifts will be tested for authenticity. When you begin to release your gift, get ready for all hell to break loose. When you decide to stop being an employed person and become a deployed person, all your "enemies" will wake up. You have to be ready for the fight and stay focused. The testing comes to prove your dedication and commitment to your gift. That's the way life is.

You need to be aware that when you start deploying yourself and working on your gift after hours, your family members or friends might say, "What are you doing?" You can tell them, "I'm working on my gift," and they may reply, "What are you talking about? You'd better go rest. You work all day." They will start talking you out of it. Yet a vision that has been tested will eventually be trusted. When I began working on my dream, none of my family members understood me. But they all ended up supporting me, and some have come to work for me.

Perhaps your vision is being tested right now. You find it difficult to do what you're doing because nobody else is doing it. You wonder why it's so hard. You have to get up at five o'clock in the morning to keep it up. You're working at a job at the same time that you're working on your dream because you know you *have* to keep working on that dream. You must pay your bills, but, at the same time, your gift has been ignited. While there will be tests, let me tell you the good news: the tests don't come to destroy your gift—they come to prove your gift. Stay with it.

GIVE YOUR SEED THE RIGHT ENVIRONMENT

You can have good seed and still be broke if your seed is not placed in the right environment. I mentioned earlier how, if you put a wheat seed on a tile floor and leave it there for twenty years, the wheat plant will remain in the seed. It's in the wrong environment for germination and growth. Similarly, if we're spending time with the wrong people, the wrong books, the wrong TV shows, and the wrong ideas, then we're placing ourselves in the wrong environment for our seed to grow and bear fruit.

I choose my friends very carefully. I have plenty of people around me but very few friends. To me, friends are fertilizer for my life and for my dreams. The wrong people in your life can be dream-killers. Just as your family members might not understand you, your friends and acquaintances might tell you that it's unrealistic for you to talk about having a dream, a vision, and a seed to sow. When they finish with you, you go right back to your old way of thinking. You have to give your mind and heart the right environment by spending time with people of vision and by reading, viewing, and thinking about things that will support the deployment of your gift.

Do you think you've been in a dry spell in your job for so long that there's nothing meaningful left for you to do in life? Have you responded to life's responsibilities by setting aside all your dreams? Do you think you're too old to cultivate your gift? Has anyone implied that your days of contributing to the world are over? Don't let discouragement or fatigue cause you to give up. What you need is the right environment—and you can cultivate the right environment for yourself to bring forth what's within your seed. Don't ever let anyone—not even yourself—write you off. Begin again to pursue your purpose. It will lead to your success.

WHICH IS MORE IMPORTANT?

I mentioned earlier that your work can become your job if you find your work *in* your job. You may drive every day or telecommute to a place of employment where you actually use your gift and are fulfilling your purpose. If you have a job where you are becoming who you are, then you are not "working a job"—you're "going to your work."

But if you have a job in which you cannot develop—or fully develop—your seed, you have to reach the point where your gift becomes more important to you than your job. When you see that there is life beyond your career, beyond your skill, you will enter into your true work, and you will become an agent of innovation and positive change in your generation.

13

FOUR STRATEGIES FOR SUCCESS IN YOUR DOMAIN

"Be fruitful and multiply;
fill ["replenish"] the earth and subdue it."[92]

In this chapter, we're going to zero in on four principles of the Creator's purpose for our success and prosperity that we can apply to our unique domain of gifting. I call it "God's economic plan."

THE ABILITY TO PRODUCE

Let's begin by addressing how can we know that God wants us to be prosperous, because people sometimes wonder about this. To address this question, let's look at the following passage from the Manufacturer's Manual:

> You may say to yourself, "My power and the strength of my hands have produced this wealth for me." But remember the LORD your God, for it is he who gives you the ability to produce wealth, and

so confirms his covenant, which he swore to your ancestors, as it is today.[93]

Let's take a close look at these statements. First, the great leader Moses told the people whom he was leading, "Remember the LORD your God, for it is he who gives you the ability to produce wealth."[94] This statement tells us *how* to become wealthy. Wealth doesn't come from God in the sense that He hands us money. Read it carefully. What does God give us? "The *ability to produce*." In the previous chapter, we began to talk about being a producer as we develop our gift. We have been given an innate ability by the Creator to generate wealth. Consequently, wealth comes from finding our ability to produce something. When we produce, we either make something, work something out, or express something. Therefore, God gave us the skills, along with the laws, that, if put into practice, will result in prosperity. This is why He says, in essence, "To be successful, go and find your gift, your ability to be prosperous."

Second, Moses told the people to be careful about how they thought about their prosperity: "But remember the LORD your God, for it is he who gives you the ability to produce wealth." God is not against our becoming prosperous. He just wants us to remember and respect where that wealth came from and to use it wisely.

BORN TO HAVE "DOMINION"

In the first book written by Moses in the Hebrew Scriptures, we find four specific strategies for being a producer by using the seed that is within us. Every successful company in the world uses these strategies—they are the system the Creator established that lets us know what we are supposed to do in order to succeed in our purpose and gifting. These strategies are at the heart of the process by which we express our true work to the world.

Earlier, we saw how God said, "Let Us make man in Our image, according to Our likeness."[95] This statement is immediately followed by a statement of purpose: "Let them have *dominion*...over all the earth."[96] The biblical narrative shows us the way in which God carried out His plan: "So God created man in His own image; in the image of God He created him; male and female He created them."[97] God gave both male and female the same instructions: have dominion. Now, God is a good God. He knows those whom He has made, and He knows why He made them, so He also tells them how to effect their purpose of dominion.

Next, we read, "Then God blessed them, and God said to them...."[98] I want to emphasize that God is communicating here. To whom is He speaking? Humans. What is He saying to them? He is giving them (and us) instructions to follow:

> Be fruitful and multiply; fill ["replenish"] the earth and subdue it; have dominion over the fish of the sea, over the birds of the air, and over every living thing that moves on the earth.[99]

These statements give us the following essential instructions for success in exercising our inherent gifting:

1. Be fruitful
2. Multiply
3. Fill, or replenish
4. Subdue

To have dominion means to impact the environment with your gifting. What this implies is that you were born to "have dominion over," or to "dominate," an area of life for which people will pay you, so that you can be personally fulfilled and financially prosperous. When you exercise this dominion, people will be eager to come to you for what you have to offer. Let's see how this transpires.

In God's instructions, the verb "be fruitful" doesn't specifically refer to having children. It means to produce something. In Hebrew, it "expresses the idea of bringing forth, branching out, or yielding increase. In Scripture it is consistently tied to the life-giving power of God."[100]

The Creator didn't tell human beings to be "seedful." Why is that? He already assumed that we had seed within us—because He put it there. Instead, He told us to be *fruitful*. Your seed is already within you, and it has life in itself; you have the ability to produce the fruit from which you're supposed to prosper. What is fruit? It is "produce." When a tree produces fruit, it is evidence that what was inside the tree is now manifest.

Now, can one piece of fruit make us prosperous? No. God says, "Go to the next level: *multiply.*" Suppose I had many crates filled with fruit sitting in a building on the grounds of my orchard. Would I be prosperous? No, I would have a lot of fruit, but I would still be broke if I didn't sell that fruit. So, even multiplying is not enough. We have to go to the third level: *replenish.*

Replenishing refers to distributing our product or service. But even if we distribute it, it might go to only a limited number of people, so we have to do something else in order to allow our gift to be prosperous. We have to move to the fourth level: *subdue.*

In this sense, the command to subdue means to control the market. What I mean by this is that, when you start distributing your product or offering your service, it needs to become prominent in the marketplace so that, whenever people want that product or service, they will think of you.

You were born to "have dominion over," or to "dominate," an area of life for which people will pay you, so that you can be personally fulfilled and financially prosperous.

BECOMING PEOPLE'S GO-TO

Let's take a simple example of international fast-food restaurants. What are they especially known for? Their signature hamburgers. Can people buy one of those hamburgers at just any store? No. People can't even recreate them at home in exactly the same way: they might buy hamburger meat, onions, buns, and everything else, but they still can't recreate the taste. This is because the company has refined their recipe; they use a specific system for making their hamburgers and their sauces. Similarly, you must refine your gift to make it distinct.

Yet creating those signature hamburgers, in themselves, didn't make these companies prosperous. They had to find a way to multiply them and their other products so that the same food was made according to the same system in every one of their restaurants. The companies trained their employees in how to make their burgers in order to maintain consistency. Then, in order to distribute their food to a wide number of customers, they established franchises.

The companies' franchises have now become so widespread that they have subdued the market for their particular signature hamburgers. If you want a specific type of hamburger, you have to drive past all the other restaurants and go to the one that has the burger you are especially looking for. Each fast-food restaurant has its own specialty items that draw their customers to select them over the others.

If you own a business or sell a product or service, do people make a point of going specifically to you for your goods or services to obtain what they want? Jesus of Nazareth said, "Whoever wants to become great among you must be your servant, and whoever wants to be first must be your slave—just as the Son of Man did not come to be served, but to serve, and to give his life as a ransom for many."[101] If you want to be great, serve your gift to the world. If you want to be first, become a "slave" to your gift—work hard on developing it. In this context, being "first" means, again, that you're the first one people think of when they want what your product or service has to offer.

I receive invitations to speak from all over the world, and I sometimes ask myself, "Why are they inviting me, when there are many other people whom they might ask instead?" The answer is that I have developed a "signature product" that they feel they can't find anywhere else. A few years ago, I received a call from T. D. Jakes, who said, "Look, Dr. Munroe, we are in a meeting here in Dallas, and we're discussing a leadership cruise, and the first name that came up was yours."

I have never invited myself to speak anywhere, whether it was at a corporation, a university, an organization, or a church. People came looking for the fruit I produced, and they invited me. I'm not teaching you something that I myself haven't done. I'm not different from you. But I was never taught this principle—I had to discover it on my own—and I want to pass it along because I desire the same results for you. I want to help you find your specialty item or service that will gain the attention of people in the marketplace so you can be successful. Produce fruit that people have to come to you for!

The individual who becomes successful and prosperous is the one whom everybody wants or needs to go to in order to get something done. Why do you go to the dentist to have your teeth cleaned or to deal with a toothache? Because your dentist made themself valuable to you by learning to perform certain dental procedures that you need to have done but can't do for yourself. Why do you go to a doctor and give them your money, regardless of the state of the economy? Because your doctor made themself valuable to you by specializing in a field of knowledge through which they can address your medical needs. Why do you take your money to a lawyer? Because your lawyer made themself valuable to you by refining their gift to meet your legal needs.

If your car breaks down, your mechanic has the technical knowledge related to repairing it, so they tell you, "I'll fix it for five hundred dollars." You say, "Five hundred dollars?!" They reply, "I know the laws of car mechanics. If you want your car to work, it'll cost five hundred dollars." What's the difference between you and your mechanic? They have the knowledge and skill to fix your car, and you lack that knowledge and skill. You see, when you develop your gift to make it distinct, offering people something that they need or want, you can demand your own value for manifesting that gift.

Here's a question to answer: Why should I come to you for your gift? How you answer that question tells me if you're going to be successful. The next question is even more difficult: Why should I give my money to you? What have you refined that would make me seek you out and pay for your product or service?

You have to realize that many people may already be doing something similar to what you're doing (or what you would like to be doing), so you can't do it in exactly the same way they do it. They have their own distinct way, so you each have a unique gift to offer. But just as a restaurant offers meals that people aren't able to imitate and therefore have to go to that specific restaurant to eat, find a way to make your product or service different from others'. When that product or service is unique and you are able to distribute it effectively, you will have "dominion."

As you begin to be fruitful and multiply your fruit, consider this: when a tree produces fruit, it is never for the tree itself. I've never seen a tree eat its own fruit, have you? Similarly, the seed within you that you were born with contains the potential for fruit, yet when that fruit is produced, it is not primarily intended for you but for others. However, you have to manifest that fruit so that others can see it and come to you for it. Trees don't bring their fruit to people. When a tree bears fruit, harvesters are attracted to it. The tree simply produces fruit, and the clients find the tree because they want what the tree has to offer. It is the fruit you produce that will attract and keep people's attention.

> *Do people make a point of going specifically to you for your goods or services to obtain what they want?*

WAYS OF "SUBDUING" THE MARKETPLACE

How can we more specifically apply the above four strategies for exercising dominion? Here are some ways to become successful in your domain and "subdue" the marketplace as you bear fruit through your gifting. These ways are applicable to both producing/distributing goods and offering services.

GIVE PEOPLE ADDED VALUE/OFFER THEM SOMETHING EXTRA

There are many ways to add value to a customer's experience, whether it is with a specific type of product, a bonus item, a particular environment, or something else—so be creative! The effort will be worth it. Be sure to keep up the quality of your primary service while giving people this "something extra." If you are a chef who owns a restaurant, you might sell your specialty sauce to customers who want to take home a taste of your cooking. Or, suppose you sell shoes, and you currently offer a basic transaction of exchanging shoes for payment. You need to find a way to add value to your store. As you sell shoes, you might offer fresh hot coffee to every customer, providing a nice corner area in which they can sit and enjoy it. That's one small example of added value. If you take care in the preparation of the coffee, and the customers like it, they may pass the word: "When you go to that store, you'll get a great cup of coffee." You're creating an environment where people want to be.

BE UNIQUE

We talked about making sure your product or service is distinct. There's something that you were born with that other people don't have in the way that you have it. So provide them with something no one else is able to give them, making it your specialty. Focus on a specific area of need that people have so that they'll come look for you. Suppose you are a beautician. Make your hairstyling services special. Perhaps obtain some extra training and study new techniques and styles, and then come back and tell people, "I'm the only one in our area who uses this technique and can offer these new hairstyles."

If you are a carpenter, focus on one area you enjoy doing, such as cabinets, and tell people, "I specialize in custom-made cabinets." That will make you stand out among other carpenters. If you just say you are a "carpenter," you will be compared to everyone else who is a carpenter. But if you are an expert at making custom cabinets, you have become valuable and significant because you have a refined gift. Or, suppose you want to open a restaurant. That can be a difficult business. People open restaurants all the time that close not long afterward. This is because many people don't just buy a sandwich; they buy a unique experience. Why should people come to your restaurant? Think about what it might offer that is unique and valuable.

I've previously shared the story about a woman who told me she felt God was directing her to open a shoe store; that was her vision. She didn't just open a general shoe store—she opened a store that sold only babies' and children's shoes. She developed one of the largest shoe stores in New Jersey. People come from various parts of the state to buy her shoes. Why? Her store is unique. When many people in that state think of babies' and children's shoes, they think of her store.

One time, my wife and I were in Monte Carlo, and we visited a clothing store. When we walked in, I saw that the rug was thick and white. In other words, don't come in here if you have dirty shoes! We were greeted by a store representative who said, "Come, please have a seat." They sat us at a beautiful glass table, and then they served us tea and cookies. Although this was a clothing store, no clothes were on display. They were hidden away upstairs.

What a store that was. We had only come to buy clothing, but they were providing a unique experience. After they had finished "wining and dining" us, they said, "Come upstairs and see our wares." Everything up there was in private little booths. The price tag on one dress was $28,000. A small purse cost $5,500. I told my wife, "You took me to the wrong store, but we already drank the tea and ate the cookies!" We felt that we had to buy something. I said, "Now, go for the cheapest thing here! Honey, come over here to this side. Walk over here." There was a belt for $400. I said, "Yes, that belt looks good!"

My point is, the store was unique. That's why people fly in from all over the world to go there just to buy one dress. The store makes thousands of dollars on one dress because they're not just selling dresses. They're selling the experience of glamour.

Your uniqueness makes you valuable, so offer people something that is distinctive to you. And even as you diversify your products or services, make sure that whatever you offer is a unique or specialized item or experience.

PROVIDE QUALITY

Sometimes quality alone is enough to enable you to stand out. Many customers want to make sure they are purchasing a product that is well made and will last, and they are willing to pay for it. What is the quality of your product? Is it sufficient to meet what your customers or potential customers are looking for?

GIVE ATTENTION TO DETAIL

Paying attention to detail is good for business. For example, if you have a store, think about how to make your product displays more attractive. Discover what your customers like and find a way to personalize the product or service for them. If you play background music in your store, check to see if the style of music is what your customers want to hear while they are shopping. Make every aspect of the customer experience special and appealing. It will keep people coming.

FOCUS ON GOOD SERVICE

Don't try to cut corners or be careless in the way you interact with people. Let people know you care about them and about what they are looking to you to provide for them. When you offer true service, it's a whole new ball game for your business.

IDENTIFY PEOPLE'S NEEDS

Finding out what people need will enable you to become a good business leader. People's needs can change over time. If someone comes to you and complains that you aren't doing something or aren't meeting a need, take that complaint seriously and consider its merit. You will always encounter individuals who complain just for the sake of it, yet some people may be expressing a real need that isn't being met but that you can remedy.

> *To have dominion means to impact the environment with your gifting.*

BE GENUINELY INTERESTED IN PEOPLE

Avoid focusing on a bottom line of trying to make money. Be genuinely interested in your clients or customers. If you do that, they'll be interested in you and what you have to offer.

Remember that you were born to solve a problem. That's where ideas for businesses come from. A business is simply a way of solving people's problems or meeting their needs. Many of us aren't looking for solutions to problems. Instead, we're looking for problems to complain about! But potential businesses are all around us because problems are all around us. When I first saw a massage chair at an airport, it was in Asia. I thought, "Something has started here." Now, almost every airport seems to offer massage chairs. Why? Because people's muscles get tight when they travel, and they need to relax. Someone recognized that problem and thought, "I can solve this," and they turned it into a lucrative business.

So, as you think about your gift, think about problems that need to be solved and how your gift ties into a solution to them. Study the problems around you. Spend a whole day just driving around looking for problems. You'll be amazed at what you see. At the same time, listen for complaints, because every complaint is also a potential business. You were given the ability to solve a problem, and I believe that anyone who solves problems can become prosperous.

14

RESPONDING TO CHALLENGING TIMES

"If there is a silver lining to bad times, it is this: When facing severe challenges, your mind normally is at its sharpest. Humans have seldom created anything of lasting value unless they were tried or hurting."
—Jon Huntsman Sr.[102]

How do we respond to challenging times—when life hits us on the blind side and we didn't expect things to go the way they did, when everything seems to be crumbling around us—so that we can keep moving forward on our journey of success? Perhaps you have experienced one of these scenarios or something like it:

- You feel like the system has spat you out with no regard for you as an individual.
- There's not enough money at the end of each month to take care of your financial obligations.

- You've completely lost your source of income, your house, your car—and it feels like you've lost your sanity too.
- Your company has shut down or your business has gone under.
- You're dealing with an illness, and the medical bills are eating away at your family's financial foundation and ability to leave an inheritance.

A crisis is a situation or an event that affects us and our environment and by which we are victimized. In the natural world, we consider a hurricane, a tornado, a tsunami, or a blizzard to be a crisis because it is a circumstance that we did not cause and over which we have no direct control. In the same way, we face crises in our life that we did not cause and cannot directly control. Put simply, a crisis is an unplanned and uncontrollable change.

There are times when we may generate a crisis for ourselves. Perhaps we mismanaged our funds, buying things that we couldn't afford and didn't need. We spent more money than we brought in, and now we are deeply in debt: that is a natural consequence that is built into our violation of a financial law. But if you lost your job because your company laid you off, you can't control that. If the number of clients in your business has suddenly dropped, so that you can't make enough money to keep things going, and you have to shut down, that's an unplanned change. Whatever the nature or origin of a crisis, it attacks our equilibrium. Under such circumstances, what should we do?

EVERY TEST IS TEMPORARY

No matter what you're facing, don't allow yourself to panic for too long. You may panic for a minute! But then let the panicking time be over because whatever difficult situation you're in, you're going to come out of it.

Nothing is permanent except for God, His laws, and His promises. Everything else changes. As a matter of fact, God promises us that nothing will remain the same: "To everything there is [only] a season, a time for every purpose under heaven."[103] Therefore, everything that you experience is only seasonal. If you're broke now, it's only a seasonal insolvency. If you've had to withdraw some investments or sell some property, it's only a temporary setback. You're going to move into a time of prosperity. You're only passing through a tough moment. If your company closed, if your business failed, then give it a good funeral and bury it, but then be prepared for a resurrection. You'll be back, because everything is only for a season. If you are laid off or fired, get ready for a seasonal change as you develop your gift. Your old boss may want to hire you back at the end of that season, but you might have your own company by then, and you can hire them!

In times of economic uncertainty, we need to stop waiting for the economy to turn around or for the government to institute an economic policy. We have our own kingdom "governmental policies," and they never change. They work every time. We can turn the economy around in our own life. There's no lack of money in the world. Wealth follows laws—it doesn't follow mere wishes. Your gift cannot be a victim of the economy, and a crisis cannot destroy it. Instead, the crisis you are experiencing may manifest your gift.

In addition, your seed or gift is never in recession. Isn't that a beautiful thought? If seeds are planted in the right environment, they're going to bring forth fruit. They're going to grow. There's something bigger than you within you. Again, ask God to show you the seed that's inside you so you can cultivate it.

The principle that there is a season for everything is one of the most important principles I have learned in life. It has helped me to understand that we are running a race, and our success is a process rather than an end. If one part of our life has ended or changed, that is not the end of our purpose or success. In times of difficulty and crisis, we need to remember that success has more to do with moving in the right direction than coming to a destination. So, again, instead of panicking, keep moving in the right direction by applying the laws of creation and manifesting the seed within you. Imagine a lighthouse with a wave breaking against it: the wave is moving, but the lighthouse remains grounded. God's laws are like a lighthouse—they never move. And like anything that has to do with success in life, coming out of a crisis is 100 percent law-based.

Laws have no crises. Gravity has no idea what's happening in your economy, and it doesn't care whether your finances are good or bad; again, if you jump off the roof of a building, gravity is going to pull you down.

Whether you are experiencing good times or difficult ones, I want you to recognize that God has built certain laws into His systems and products—including you—that guarantee their function, in order to protect His reputation, confirming that what He has made is good and functions well.

It doesn't matter what the issues in our life are, or what the culture is doing, or what the current fads may be; if we know laws and principles, we will overcome our circumstances. We must live by those laws and principles rather than by our feelings. Of course, we have feelings, but we are not guided by those feelings when challenges arise.

Whatever you are facing, you can say to God, "Deliver me for Your name's sake. Do it for Your own reputation." When I have a need, I say, "Lord, this isn't good for You. I will tell everybody how You provided for me." My needs keep being met. That's what I meant when I wrote earlier about "putting pressure" on God because our success is good for our Creator.

In times of difficulty and crisis, we need to remember that success has more to do with moving in the right direction than coming to a destination.

TESTS CREATE CREDIBILITY

The test we are undergoing now will create credibility for our life and will build trust in other people toward us. If you're experiencing a bankruptcy moment, that's a test to see if you can be trusted on the other side of the crisis. Never think that a crisis comes to end your life. It comes to give trustworthiness to it. No matter what you're going through, the resilience you show and the constructive responses you manifest in the midst of your troubles will earn you the respect of those who are observing you during that trial.

This brings us back to one of the laws we talked about earlier: you don't trust a product that hasn't been tested. People are looking for those who are unafraid to bring out their gift and to persevere with the plans they believe in, even—or especially—in the midst of difficulty. My organization used to be called a fly-by-night phenomenon that wouldn't last, but we survived that criticism. You are never trusted for the things you claim. You are always trusted for the things you have survived.

Some people will hope that you fail, and then, when you make it, they will congratulate you! Consequently, don't listen to the naysayers. Accept the test as part of your becoming a successful person. Successful people always have survival testimonies. They weren't born successful. Success comes to people as a result of their having survived being criticized and attacked, of their having survived the test of the fiery furnace of life, knowing that God is always with them,[104] of their having survived being thrown into a pit with lions.[105] Success is what people think of you *after* they try to kill you!

So, I encourage you to get ready for the test. People will trust you for what you have survived. Sometimes, you will never be completely accepted until you've first been completely rejected.

BENEFITS OF A CRISIS

Besides winning us credibility, there are other benefits that can come as a result of a crisis that enable us to fulfill our purpose in life. I love this statement by Shakespeare, the great playwright: "Sweet are the uses of adversity."[106] That's a deep statement. Shakespeare caught on to something. He realized that adversity can benefit the one experiencing the hardship. He's telling us that when things are adverse, when things are in crisis, we can use them to attain a positive outcome. Everything that happens to you can be used to produce something good.[107]

The following principles of crisis will lead you to success and prosperity in the midst of difficulty. Some of these areas interact or overlap with one another, yet each addresses a distinct outcome from which we can profit.

CRISIS IS THE INCUBATOR OF CREATIVITY

Most of the time, we don't think in creative ways and in new patterns until something negative happens to us. When things fall apart, it makes us think outside the box. A crisis demands innovative thinking. It makes us think about things in ways we have never thought about them before. Consider this: after God created Adam, He didn't give him a finished table or a chair. He gave Adam (and his descendants) trees, in which tables and chairs were "hidden," and He essentially said, "Work with that."

When has a crisis forced you to think about something in a fresh way? How could thinking creatively help you with a current difficulty in your life?

CRISIS DEMANDS A NEW WAY OF THINKING ABOUT OLD PROBLEMS

Here is what I mean by "old problems." Suppose you have a long-standing need to pay your mortgage each month. If you are laid off or fired from your job, the issue is that the source of income with which you used to pay your mortgage has dried up—but the old problem hasn't gone away. You still have to pay installments on your mortgage. You are therefore compelled to think in a new way in order to figure out how you can generate income to pay for the old problem.

What "old problem" do you currently have to approach in a new way? How can you find alternate means to address it?

CRISIS PUSHES US TO GROW AND IMPROVE OURSELVES

Sometimes, we become stuck in one place for too long, and the only way for us to get where we need to be is for something to happen that pushes us to a new place. We often don't grow until we are stretched to do so. Thus, a crisis can result in our making an effort to improve ourselves in some way and to activate more of our potential than we otherwise would have.

The problem with human beings is that we are creatures of habit. We need to break patterns that hold us back. Again, many of us have a habit of going to a certain workplace and thinking of it as our only option. Yet if something happens so that we are no longer employed at our job, we are compelled to look around for new opportunities. Or we may have a habit of being broke all the time. Even when we do have money, we end up spending it just to make sure we are broke again because being without money feels familiar to us. If we experience an extreme financial crisis in our life, that pattern can be interrupted because we come to a place where we and our family members need to survive, and we start implementing sound financial principles to get through the emergency. The experience shows us the benefits of following those principles consistently in our lives.

If you are currently facing a crisis, what occasions for personal growth and the creation of new patterns do you see?

CRISIS CHALLENGES EXPERIENCE

Life has a way of shaking loose areas of our life that we thought would always stay the same. When a crisis comes, some of your past experience, skills, and ways of doing thing may become useless. What do you do when things you previously knew and depended on are no longer working for you? Experience can sometimes be your worst enemy if you have been doing something in a certain way but the environment has changed and your previous know-how is no longer relevant or needed. Sometimes we become so hooked on our past experience that we wait and wait to see if there is somewhere that we can still use our experience, but it never comes. If you are going through something like this, you may have to retool yourself, relearn some things, or gain new skills. Perhaps you have never performed a certain job before, but it has become necessary for you to learn how to do it in order to support yourself or to move forward in your purpose. Will you accept that challenge?

There are some people who are so proud that they end up starving. Someone might say, "I can't do that job. It's below me." Oh, yes? We may soon need to bury them if they don't get their act together and put their pride in their pocket. We can come out of anything, but if we idly sit at home, we aren't activating the laws that can make us prosperous. If a job opens up, we should say to ourselves, "I'm going to take it for a season." Then, we can apply the principle of "Success after 5:00" to develop our true work again. Remember, Jesus was temporarily a carpenter. He always knew that He was the Savior of the world, but until He manifested His purpose at age thirty, He had to function in a job.

Has your environment changed so that some of your past experience or skills are no longer relevant, and your holding on to them is keeping you from success? In what ways could you retool yourself in this new environment?

CRISIS GENERATES DEVELOPMENT

Jon Huntsman Sr. wrote, "If there is a silver lining to bad times, it is this: When facing severe challenges, your mind normally is at its sharpest. Humans have seldom created anything of lasting value unless they were tried or hurting." Let's talk about two statements within this quote. First, Huntsman said that when you are experiencing the biggest trials, this is when your mind is normally at its sharpest. Your mind is in crisis mode and has to think of things it has never thought of before. Second, he said, "Humans seldom have created anything of lasting value unless they were tried or hurting." He was speaking from experience, saying that we don't produce anything of note unless we are under pressure. Therefore, when we face a crisis, it forces us to develop new approaches to life and to the process of living. Probably every progressive invention came out of a problem. That's because a crisis makes us imagine unique approaches, and this leads to our developing solutions and innovative ways of doing things.

What is something beneficial that you could develop or produce in response to the pressure you are experiencing?

> *A crisis makes us imagine unique approaches, and this leads to our developing solutions and innovative ways of doing things.*

CRISIS CREATES NEW OPPORTUNITIES

With new ways of doing things and new inventions come new opportunities, industries, fields of endeavor, and reforms. What opportunities for progress do you recognize in your life and in the world around you? What new industries and activities do you see in your community and nation that fit your gifting?

CRISIS MANIFESTS TRUE LEADERSHIP ABILITY

No matter how much someone might claim to be a leader, only when they experience a challenging time can they *prove* that they are a leader. You are not really a leader in good times. While everyone has leadership potential within them, genuine leadership is tested and verified in a crisis environment.

A crisis tests whether we are as mature as we claim to be. Perhaps we've been telling people how good God has been to us. Do we still make the same claim when things fall apart in our lives? Or perhaps we've been expressing to others how much faith we have. Let's see what kind of faith we have when we are in a situation where things don't look very good and we wonder how we're going to make it to the next day.

How do your leadership ability and principles hold up when you are under pressure?

CRISIS IGNITES A PASSION FOR A RENEWED VISION

Sometimes we stray from our purpose, and God has to pull the rug out from under us to get us back on track. Often, a crisis will make us stop and reflect on the original idea that the Creator revealed to us. It will prompt us to return to our true passion and vision.

Are you on track with your purpose and gift?

BACK TO THE BASICS: GENEROSITY AND THANKFULNESS

If you are experiencing any form of challenge or crisis in your life, consider carefully how you might glean from it lessons and opportunities that can benefit you. At the same time, focus on some of the basics in life that will sustain you. Among those basics are the practices of generosity and thankfulness. Sometimes we make things complicated and try to work things out and calculate what we need to do next when the best thing we can do is to look away from our problems for the moment and look toward helping other people.

Solomon wrote, "The generous will themselves be blessed, for they share their food with the poor."[108] And Jesus taught, "Give, and it will be given to you. A good measure, pressed down, shaken together and running over, will be poured into your lap. For with the measure you use, it will be measured to you."[109] If you are having financial difficulty, you might not have much money to give away, but what else might you give to someone? It could be as simple as offering your time and your tools to a neighbor's building project, donating canned food from your own pantry to a food drive, or baking someone a cake.

There might be other things that you can share with others as well. Think creatively. For example, perhaps you use your car mainly to drive to work. Why not put it to use serving people, such as giving an older person a ride to the grocery store or to a doctor's appointment? By doing this, you will be activating a law: "Give, and it will be given to you."

Thousands of years ago, one of the psalmists wrote this timeless truth: "Give thanks to the Lord, for he is good; his love endures forever."[110] You can give God thanks for what He will do to show you your purpose and to bring you out of your difficulties for His name's sake. God has said, "I know the plans I have for you,...plans to prosper you and not to harm you, plans to give you hope and a future."[111] He says He has a plan to give us hope, so He has to make sure we make it to the fruit-bearing stage. He has to make sure we make it to our destiny because His name is on the line. God is going to make you successful for His name's sake. He's going to fix things because of His reputation. Hope is coming.

Let's remember that Matthew, one of Jesus's disciples, reported Jesus as saying, "Seek first his kingdom and his righteousness, and all these things will be given to you as well."[112] Luke the physician, another disciple, reports the same saying of Jesus: "But seek his kingdom, and these things will be given to you as well. Do not be afraid, little flock, for your Father has been pleased to give you the kingdom."[113]

Seek first the kingdom of God, and these things will be what? "Given to you as well." What "things"? The answer is whatever provision you need to live and to fulfill your purpose—in times of peace and in times of crisis—leading to your success.

PART FOUR

DEVELOPING AN ENVIRONMENT FOR SUCCESS

15

TEN KEYS FOR PERSONAL SUCCESS, PART 1

"Through imagination, we can visualize the uncreated worlds of potential that lie within us. Through conscience, we can come in contact with universal laws or principles with our own singular talents and avenues of contribution, and with the personal guidelines within which we can most effectively develop them."
—Stephen R. Covey[114]

In this section of the book, we will further discuss how to personally develop an environment for our success. I have found it helpful to encapsulate many of the concepts and principles I teach about success into "Ten Keys for Personal Success" so that they can stay in the forefront of our mind and we can be daily reminded to put them into practice. These keys both reinforce and expand on themes we have discussed so far. In this chapter, we will cover the first five keys—*purpose, perception, potential, passion,* and *principles*—and in the next chapter, we will explore the last five—*plan, people, persistence, perseverance,* and *prayer.* All ten keys start with the letter *p* so that we can more easily remember them.

KEY 1: PURPOSE

I can't emphasize this point enough: to be successful, you *must* start by having a personal sense of purpose—an awareness of the reason for your existence. We have seen that our purpose is the original intent of the Manufacturer—the God of creation—for us. Without a clear idea of your purpose, you can't start the process of success because success means accomplishing the purpose you were put on earth to fulfill. Every human being was created to make a specific contribution to this world, and it is when we discover our purpose that we can begin to find true success and prosperity.

The seed of our success is hidden in our purpose and in the gift we have been given to carry out that purpose. If you haven't yet begun to actively seek out your purpose and the specific contribution you were destined to make to your generation, I urge you to begin doing so today.

KEY 2: PERCEPTION

This key is based on the principle that you can't follow a path that you can't see. I like to say that having perception, or vision, is "seeing your purpose in pictures"—in other words, having a clear conception of where you are going.

God gave humanity the gift of perception so that we would not have to live only by what we see but would also have the ability to imagine what *can be* and to make it a reality. We know that our purpose is already "finished" and that God has placed within us the potential for fulfilling it. And we see our purpose through faith. To paraphrase the writer of the book of Hebrews, faith is the substance of things you hope to accomplish, the evidence of things you can see even when others cannot.[115] When you lack perception—when you don't have a vision for your future and destiny—you will likely relive the past with its disappointments and failures. Only by seeing what is not yet here can you bring something new, creative, and exciting into existence.

Thus, it doesn't matter what you currently have or don't have, as long as you can see what you *could* have. Perception is a key to success because where there's a dream, there's hope, and where there's hope, there's faith.

Everything we do—the way we conduct our entire life—should be guided by our perception of the purpose God has placed in our heart. It must influence what we spend our time and money on and what our priorities are. Without perception, we will lack values to guide our living. Our life will have no sense of direction, our activities will have no meaning, our time will have no purpose, and our resources will have no application.

> *God gave humanity the gift of perception so that we would not have to live only by what we see but would also have the ability to imagine what can be and to make it a reality.*

KEY 3: POTENTIAL

The third key is that you must understand your potential. This is directly related to your perception, in which you imagine what can be. You must believe in your potential to reach the fulfillment of your dream more than other people's assessment of you or what the "odds" look like. Otherwise, you will never be successful.

Potential is hidden capacity, untapped power, unreleased energy. It is all that you could be but haven't yet become. It is who you really are, even if you don't yet know your true self. You must come into an awareness of this capacity within you.

Know that your ability isn't dependent on what you perceive as your limitations. How many people have made statements such as these: "I don't have a good education"; "I don't have the money to start a business"; "No one in my family has ever done anything like this"; "I'm part of a minority group"; "I don't have the right connections"; "I'm too young"; "I'm past my prime"; "I'm scared I'll fail"? People often have a long list of reasons why they can't do what they dream of doing. None of those excuses is valid. Why? Because your potential is determined by the purpose and gift God has given you, not by anything else.

Whatever you were born to do, you are equipped to do. Moreover, resources will become available to you as you need them. Whatever God is calling you to dream is a revelation of your ability. What this means is that God gives ability to fulfill responsibility. God would never give you an assignment without also granting you the facility to undertake it and the provision for it—either now or at a later time when it is needed. Prosperity doesn't mean that tomorrow's need is met today; it means that today's need is met today. Therefore, when you begin to move forward with your dream, you will uncover your ability and your provision.

When you understand this principle, no one can stop you from being successful. God has created you to do something wonderful, and you have genuine potential to fulfill that purpose.

KEY 4: PASSION

Passion is also birthed from perception—from a revelation of where you are headed in life. Every great man or woman became great because they possessed the spirit of passion. Yet I believe that the majority of the people in the world lack true passion for living. I think that passion is rare in human experience.

Passion may be defined in the following ways:

- *A deep desire.* Passion is stamina that says, "I'm going to go after this, no matter what happens. If I have to wait five, ten, or fifteen years, I will get it." If you want to go all the way to your dream, you can't sit back and expect everything to be easy. People who are successful possess a deep desire that produces a passion in them to proceed with their dreams. Does your desire for what you would like to do have stamina?
- *An obligation.* When you are passionate about something, you feel compelled to do it. Passion will enable you to stand against and to overcome opposition, resistance, criticism, and all other obstacles to manifesting your gift. Do you feel that you *must* activate your gift and achieve your purpose?
- *An intense commitment.* Many people are interested in doing certain things, but they aren't really committed to doing them. The

world is filled with people who are interested but lack zeal. Those who are successful are willing to put their whole self into accomplishing their dream. Passionate people are those who have discovered something more important than life itself. Are you willing to pay the price to obtain what you desire?

- *A profound resolution.* Those who attain personal success are resolved in their decision to pursue their purpose, gifting, and goals. How determined are you? Have you truly resolved to fulfill your purpose?
- *A clear motivation.* Passion is the juice for living. For many people, life is a drudgery. They have no motivation in regard to their job, spouse, education, or personal development. Having a clear motivation in life helps us to rise above our daily routine. Are you just existing, or are you pursuing a reason for living? Do you have an inner motivation to follow your dream?

When the Creator's purpose for you is so vivid that you can see it in your mind's eye, then that mental picture will create within you an enthusiasm to fulfill it. It will ignite within you a deep desire to make your unique contribution to this world. You know that you have tapped into your potential for success when you are so actively involved in the things you want to do that you can't stop thinking about them and working on them.

Passion also helps us to stay focused on our purpose. And it is only when we have a passion for what we desire to do that things start happening to enable us to fulfill it. Passion ignites results.

> *People who are successful possess a deep desire that produces a passion in them to proceed with their dreams.*

KEY 5: PRINCIPLES

In section 2, we explored the origin and nature of the Manufacturer's laws and principles—and our vital need to align our life with them in our journey of success. After the Manufacturer created human beings, He gave them valuable information about how they functioned, how to properly operate their life, and how to ensure that they would be successful. He conveyed specific principles so they could understand the nature by which they had been designed to live. Later on in human history, He made sure that these principles, as well as additional instructions, were put into writing as a vital reference for all of humanity. The laws and principles contained in the biblical record are time-tested and stable. When we follow these laws and principles, we protect and preserve our vision and passion.

We have looked at the similarities and differences between natural laws and spiritual laws. Following spiritual laws will lead us to success in practical matters—such as the best way to handle finances, business matters, and relationships—as well as in moral ones. Spiritual laws enable us to know how to respond in constructive ways to everyday, real-world challenges related to exercising our gift and also to ethical issues that we will inevitably face along the way. For example, the book of Proverbs gives much practical wisdom that we can apply in a number of situations. One passage, which uses an example from the natural world, addresses the risks of laziness and the rewards of working to provide for our own needs:

> Go to the ant, you sluggard; consider its ways and be wise! It has no commander, no overseer or ruler, yet it stores its provisions in summer and gathers its food at harvest. How long will you lie there, you sluggard? When will you get up from your sleep? A little sleep, a little slumber, a little folding of the hands to rest—and poverty will come on you like a thief and scarcity like an armed man.[116]

In another section of the Manufacturer's Manual, Jesus of Nazareth discusses our need to address our own shortcomings before trying to correct others' faults:

> Why do you look at the speck of sawdust in your brother's eye and pay no attention to the plank in your own eye? How can you say to your brother, "Brother, let me take the speck out of your eye," when you yourself fail to see the plank in your own eye? You

> hypocrite, first take the plank out of your eye, and then you will see clearly to remove the speck from your brother's eye.[117]

Perhaps you are building a business or providing a service, but you have been ignoring time-honored principles from the Manufacturer. Through your charismatic personality and enthusiasm, you have gotten people excited about following you and contributing to your work. But, underneath, your foundation is not secure. Your organization or endeavor may grow at first. Yet when it gets to a certain point, it will stop expanding because you haven't applied the principles necessary for it to grow beyond that point. The growth of a business or service is not all about strategic business plans, astute investments, and talented employees. You also have to conduct your business or other work honestly, make wise decisions, and hire people with integrity—those who have a passion for the corporate vision and who value and support the contributions of all their coworkers.

Committing—or recommitting—to the Creator's laws and principles is like rebooting a stalled computer by pushing the reset button: it allows us to return to the "original mode" where we can function as we were intended to. By studying and implementing these principles, you will avoid moral compromise and ethical missteps. You will protect yourself from the negative effects that such mistakes inevitably have on other aspects of your life, including the exercise of your gifts and the realization of your potential. You will be able to say, with the biblical writer, "I will walk about in freedom, for I have sought out your precepts."[118] We will talk further in a coming chapter about how to establish an ethical foundation for our life as the underpinning for success, discussing how we can determine and write out the core principles by which we will live and conduct ourselves.

In the next chapter, we will explore the final five keys for personal success, beginning with specific guidelines for making a plan to carry out our assignment in life.

16

TEN KEYS FOR PERSONAL SUCCESS, PART 2

"Life is a splendid gift. There is nothing small in it.
Far the greatest things grow by God's law out of the smallest.
But to live your life, you must discipline it."
—Florence Nightingale[119]

When you apply to your life the ten essential keys we are looking at, they will all work together to create a fruitful atmosphere and a secure framework that will enable you to succeed. Each key is significant and distinct, and supports the others. Let us now consider the final keys: *plan, people, persistence, perseverance,* and *prayer.*

KEY 6: PLAN

Those who are successful develop a clear plan for what they desire to do. I've known people who have tried to be successful over and over again without having a plan. It doesn't work. Jesus said that a wise person doesn't start to build something unless they first work out the details:

> Suppose one of you wants to build a tower. Won't you first sit down and estimate the cost to see if you have enough money to complete it? For if you lay the foundation and are not able to finish it, everyone who sees it will ridicule you, saying, "This person began to build and wasn't able to finish."[120]

I'm a stickler for planning. Anyone who works with me will tell you that. One of the reasons I continually emphasize that we need to know and focus on our purpose is because plans that don't help us fulfill our purpose are counterproductive to our life. But if we follow a plan based on our purpose, then that plan can unfold, and what we desire to do can become a reality.

Solomon wrote, "To humans belong the plans of the heart, but from the LORD comes the proper answer of the tongue."[121] That's a very powerful statement. God is saying, in effect, "I gave you your purpose and gift, as well as the perception to see your purpose in pictures. Now, you put the plan on paper, and I will work out the details." Solomon added, "In their hearts humans plan their course, but the LORD establishes their steps."[122] If we don't have a plan, how can God direct us?

Do you have a plan? Do you know what you want to do next week, next month, next year, five years from now? Do you have a plan for the next twenty years of your life? Can you give me a plan for your life for the next fifty years? God has given you the ability to do that. He has given you a mind, the gift of imagination, and the vision of faith. What are you waiting for? There may be people close to you who don't understand what you're dreaming, but put your dream on paper anyway. Why? Your dream is worth fleshing out and writing down. If God gave you the dream, it deserves to be done. God says He will explain how your plan will be accomplished, yet He can't discuss it with you until you have something concrete to talk about.

Ask yourself what practical steps you need to take to reach your dream. You must answer and take action on questions such as these for the success of your plan:

1. What do I want to accomplish?
2. Who do I need?

3. What do I have?
4. Where can I go for information?
5. What should I read?
6. What courses or what type of education might be helpful or necessary?
7. With whom should I associate?
8. How long should it take?
9. How much will it cost?
10. Where can I get experience?

You may need to adjust or refine the specifics of your plan as God leads you through the process of its fulfillment, but you first need to identify and clarify where you are headed so that you can begin. You can use the following process:

Identify

Clarify

Refine

Document

Articulate

Communicate

Demonstrate

Reevaluate

Revise

Repeat

Besides having a general plan, you need to set goals and objectives in relation to your plan so that you can be ready to carry it out. A goal may be defined as:

- An established point of achievement that leads to a greater accomplishment
- A point of measure for progress toward an ultimate purpose

- A prerequisite for the achievement of an ultimate plan

Success comes from the discipline of setting goals according to your purpose. Goals give us a structure for completing our plan one step at a time. They give us a starting place and an ending place, and they help us to focus. Where you end up in life is a result of the goals that you set or do not set. If you don't have any goals for yourself, other people will run your life. And the more successful you become, the more people will compete for your time, so you have to guard your goals even more carefully then. Those who are successful are always zealous for and jealous of their goals because these goals represent their lives. When our goals change, our lives change.

After you establish your goals, you should write out your objectives, which are a detailed breakdown of your goals. They determine when you want things to happen. You must clearly delineate what you need to do and when you need to do it in order to get to where you want to go. Objectives should include specific timetables.

To fulfill your plan, it is necessary not only to discipline yourself to follow your goals and objectives but also to seek wise counsel. At any stage of life, it is a good practice for us to seek the counsel of two or three people whom we trust before making a major decision, carefully listening to and weighing their answers according to our personal vision and values. Solomon wrote, "Plans fail for lack of counsel, but with many advisers they succeed."[123]

> *Your dream is worth fleshing out and writing down.*
> *If God gave you the dream, it deserves to be done.*

KEY 7: PEOPLE

The seventh key, people, refers to the fact that you must guard yourself from the wrong people while gathering around yourself the right people. Having the right people in your life means being around those who will support you in your goals—those who will partner with you and influence you to reach them. In contrast, having the wrong people around you is dangerous because they will pull you away from your purpose and from success.

When thinking about the people in your life, consider the law of association. This law states that *you become like those with whom you spend time.* We often underestimate others' influence on us. We don't know we're being influenced by them until it is too late. Since your purpose can be either encouraged or undermined by others, you must be careful whom you allow to impact your life. People have the potential to create your environment. Your environment then determines your mindset, and your mindset determines your future. Thus, you must choose your friends and associates judiciously, selecting those who are truly with you and not against you.

You should generally choose friends who are going in the same direction as you and who want to obtain the same things you do so that you can reinforce one another. Here are some questions to ask yourself:

- With whom am I spending time?
- What effect are these people having on me?
- Is the effect these people are having on me a good thing in relation to my purpose?

We all need to answer these questions honestly and regularly on our journey of success.

In addressing the consequences that come with the law of association, I have had to learn to take the following three actions to protect my purpose:

1. *Disassociation.* There are people and places that you are going to have to disassociate yourself from if you're going to make it to your dream. This reality shouldn't be taken lightly. You have to disassociate yourself from people who aren't going anywhere and don't want to go anywhere in life. Some people sacrifice their dreams and even their lives because they are afraid of conflict and of disagreeing with others. Don't be afraid to disassociate yourself from people who aren't right for you. Disassociation doesn't have to be confrontational. Sometimes, you can ease out of people's lives very quietly, just as you eased into them. Disassociation is not an easy action to take, but it is a very important priority in life.

2. *Limited association.* You may not want to completely disassociate yourself from some of the people in your life. However, it is important that you thoughtfully determine how much time you will spend with people. Sometimes, we need to pull away from the undue influence of even those whom we love if we're going to follow our God-given purpose. Moreover, it's fine to have casual friends as long as you give them casual time. Perhaps there are some people you will just want to be acquainted with so that you can back off and leave them alone again if you see that being with them causes your commitment to your purpose to waver.

3. *Expanded association.* You protect your mental environment by spending major time with positive influences and minor time with negative influences. Therefore, to be successful, you need to increase the time you spend with people who have the same philosophy, goals, and discipline that you do, people who exhibit the kind of character and vision that you desire to have. These are the people with whom you want to expand your relationships. Ask yourself these questions: Who can help me toward my goal? Who can I get close to and learn from?

Key 7 also has this component: although we each receive a personal purpose and gift, we were not created to fulfill our vision by ourselves. Our gift will attract others who will contribute toward the completion of our dream. Other people help us to make it in life. Individual purpose is always fulfilled within a larger or corporate purpose. It is not God's method to give a particular assignment or vision to a group. He gives a unique vision to an individual who then shares their vision with the group and transfers it to them. The members of the group then run with the vision because they find in it a place for their own personal visions to be fulfilled. This is how God weaves personal and corporate vision together.

It's important for us to be able to work with others to make our vision a reality. We all need other people to guide, help, and encourage us along the path to fulfilling our purpose. God has people prepared to work with you, and they will be of great benefit to you. When you are acting on your dream, people will always be there, waiting to help you. Yet, if you do not yet know your purpose, or if you do not begin to act on it, the people who are supposed to help you won't know where to find you.

KEY 8: PERSISTENCE

We need to develop the quality of persistence because there will inevitably be various forms of resistance as we move toward accomplishing our purpose. There will be those who don't believe in us or what we are doing. Get used to it. It's part of the process of attaining success. This means that you have to fight to achieve your dream. Dreams don't come to you—you go for them. Like potential and passion, persistence springs from perception, or vision. Once you know what you really want and can "see" it, then, no matter what comes against you, you never give up.

Persistence may be defined as:

- The ability to face defeat again and again and not give up
- The knack for pushing on in the face of difficulty, knowing that victory is yours
- The determination to work hard at overcoming every obstacle and to do whatever is necessary to reach your goals

When we are persistent, this is a manifestation that we hold a strong conviction about our future based on the purpose God has given us for our life. As we talked about in key 4, passion, we feel that the attainment of our purpose is not optional but is an obligation and a necessity, so we would never think of abandoning our goal.

Jesus told a parable that encourages us in that it shows how success comes to those who persist—not only in the natural realm but also in the spiritual realm:

> Suppose you have a friend, and you go to him at midnight and say, "Friend, lend me three loaves of bread; a friend of mine on a journey has come to me, and I have no food to offer him." And suppose the one inside answers, "Don't bother me. The door is already locked, and my children and I are in bed. I can't get up and give you anything." I tell you, even though he will not get up and give you the bread because of friendship, yet because of your shameless audacity he will surely get up and give you as much as you need. So I say to you: Ask and it will be given to you; seek and you will find; knock and the door will be opened to you. For everyone who asks

> receives; the one who seeks finds; and to the one who knocks, the door will be opened.[124]

Thus, as long as a person can hold on to their vision, there is always a chance for them to move out of their present circumstances and toward the fulfillment of their purpose. When you know your purpose in pictures, you know how to stay in the race and complete it.

> *Once you know what you really want and can "see" it, then, no matter what comes against you, you never give up.*

KEY 9: PERSEVERANCE

Persistence and perseverance are related: one definition of *persevere* is "to persist in a state, enterprise, or undertaking in spite of counterinfluences, opposition, or discouragement."[125] However, each of these qualities makes a distinct contribution to our success. While being persistent generally means to keep pushing forward, persevering essentially means to bear up under pressure. Perseverance is the power to endure, to hold on, in spite of everything. Again, when you begin to act on your gifting, it will stir up both those who want to help you and those who want to hinder you. Opposition is often proof that you're really doing something with your life.

Although, as you pursue your purpose, you may continue to get knocked down, when you persevere, you get up again each time and dust yourself off, saying, "I'm going to start again. I'm going to try one more time—two more times, ten more times." In the 2012 Olympics held in London, there were four young Bahamian men who ran the men's 4x400 relay race and won the gold medal. This was the first Olympic men's gold medal in any sport for the Bahamas. Most people watching the Olympics only saw these four young athletes compete on television. They never witnessed their training habits or knew their history. The oldest one among them, Chris Brown, had tried and failed to win a gold medal many times, but he kept coming back and finally reached his dream.[126]

What about you? Do you keep coming back when life gets difficult? William Feather said, "Success seems to be a matter of hanging on after others have let go."[127]

I believe that we all love a winner because, deep in our DNA, in the heart of our being, is the spirit of a creature who knows how to succeed. That is why, when we see success, we identify with it. Remember that you are here on earth because you are already a winner. You began life with what it takes to fulfill your purpose. You can be hopeful because success is predictable, and your future is inevitable. If you persevere in following the laws of creation, you will succeed because your success is good for God.

Perseverance is also necessary because, as I mentioned previously, we often have to develop our gift for a long time before we are paid for it. Don't let that deter you—just keep working on your gift. Some people want to be great right away, but they need to start small. Practice your gift at every opportunity. Work your gift. Persevere.

KEY 10: PRAYER

The tenth key for personal success refers to our need for spiritual reserves. To be successful, we must have a daily relationship with our Creator. That's what prayer is. To pray is to constantly stay connected to, and to petition, the Source of our purpose and gifting. We need to go to the One who gave us our gift to receive strength and guidance to deploy it. In the next chapter, we'll talk about what it means to connect with our Source in the development of our personal character.

Earlier, we talked about the need to be alone and to quiet our life in order to discover our gift. In the book of Isaiah, the Creator says, "I make known the end from the beginning."[128] In other words, "I show you who you have been from the beginning." So, again, if you are seeking your purpose, why not spend a little time away from other people? You might go on a walk and ask the Creator to come with you. He wants to reveal or reinforce your true purpose and gift. Say, "God, let's go on a gift-finding walk." Then, regularly stay connected to Him as He reveals that purpose to you.

Additionally, regularly read the Manufacturer's Manual, which will help to guide you in your prayers. And read it not only as a devotional book but also in order to learn and remind yourself of the laws and principles of creation. Ask God to show you His laws, and then act on what you learn. We can follow the example of King David, who prayed:

> Teach me, Lord, the way of your decrees,
> that I may follow it to the end.
> Give me understanding, so that I may keep your law
> and obey it with all my heart.
> Direct me in the path of your commands,
> for there I find delight.
> Turn my heart toward your statutes
> and not toward selfish gain.
> Turn my eyes away from worthless things;
> preserve my life according to your word.
> Fulfill your promise to your servant,
> so that you may be feared.
> Take away the disgrace I dread,
> for your laws are good.
> How I long for your precepts!
> In your righteousness preserve my life.[129]

17

PROTECTING YOUR SUCCESS

"Character, in the long run, is the decisive factor in the life of an individual and of nations alike."
—Theodore Roosevelt[130]

As you pursue your purpose and experience success, don't expect your success to carry you in life.

That might seem like a surprising statement, so let me explain what I mean: Many people can't handle achievement well because the accompanying responsibility, rewards, and stakes weigh too heavily on them. People can fall into all kinds of moral and ethical problems when they are successful because they suddenly feel all-powerful and unrestrained. They don't realize that they are setting themselves up for a disastrous fall. Your gift is never a threat to your success—but a lack of character is. Throughout history, many leaders who failed did not fail because they were short on gifts but because they were short on character.

A person who has talent but lacks character can be unstable and unreliable. Some people have ability, but they don't have "availability." They're gifted, but they can't be counted on to contribute their gift consistently. Nothing is more frustrating to people who are involved in a joint endeavor than dealing with a member of the group who is extremely talented but undependable. They cannot predict if the person will be present—physically or otherwise—to carry out their responsibilities. If the person doesn't show up, the endeavor can be jeopardized.

Talent without character is like a shooting star. It shines brightly for a moment but then is gone. Sometimes, people come on the public scene who have a brilliant intellect, a sparkling personality, or dazzling good looks. They seem to have all the right ingredients for success. But then, sometime later—it may be two weeks, a year, or several years—they seem to drop out of sight, and we wonder where they went. We find out that they quickly burned out due to a character issue that destroyed their reputation and potential.

In contrast, character is like the sun—it shines consistently and reliably. On days when we experience cloudy skies or pouring rain, the sun is still shining from its consistent position in the solar system. People with character have these qualities of consistency and reliability. Consequently, they have a positive effect on the lives of those around them.

Attaining true success is thus not just about exercising the gift the Creator has implanted within us and attracting financial prosperity but also about having the character of the Creator who made us. His character and His laws go together. The only way to protect what you hope to accomplish in your life, and what you have already accomplished, is to develop and maintain strong personal character. Character development produces within us an internal environment for success.

Attaining true success is not just about exercising the gift the Creator has implanted within us and attracting financial prosperity but also about having the character of the Creator who made us.

IN SYNC WITH THE CREATOR

Jesus of Nazareth said, "What good will it be for someone to gain the whole world, yet forfeit their soul? Or what can anyone give in exchange for their soul?"[131] In effect, a person can "gain the world" through the power and riches associated with success but, at the same time, forfeit their soul—the very core of their being—by ignoring or betraying their own character. In doing so, they can lose their impact and their longevity—not to mention the reason for their very existence. That is a tragic waste of life.

For example, if we violate the laws of the Creator in our relationships with other people, we can shut down our seed of success. Success is holistic. All the laws and principles work together. Concerning relationships, Jesus said, "If you are offering your gift [to God] at the altar and there remember that your brother or sister has something against you, leave your gift there in front of the altar. First go and be reconciled to them; then come and offer your gift."[132] Therefore, if our relationships with other people are not right, we can't walk around saying, "I'm exercising the principle of giving, but I'm not receiving." That's not the issue. The issue is, do you see the whole picture, and are you applying it?

It is like planting a seed in the ground and then pouring kerosene on it once it begins to grow. You may have used sound principles of development such as providing the seed with soil, water, and light, but now you are doing something that negates the effect of those principles. When we aren't experiencing success or our success begins to wane, the reason could be as simple as the negation of a principle.

Our whole life has to be in sync with the Creator's laws and principles. That's why I can't afford to hold anything against anyone. If people insult me, I need to protect my heart and forgive them. This is the reason Jesus told us to love our enemies.[133] We love our enemies because we don't want hatred or a desire for revenge to shut down our relationships, impacting our purpose and our journey of success. I will never get in a fight with anyone because I have to guard my relationship with the Creator and allow my own tree to grow. How others respond to me is their own responsibility. I need to focus on what I'm supposed to do. Sometimes we think that when we forgive someone, they're supposed to forgive us also. That's not what the Manufacturer's Manual says. It just says we are to forgive them.[134] To forgive means to release the other person. That means the issue is now on them. You are clear in your relationship with them and with the Creator.

CHARACTER BEFORE POWER

Why is having consistently good character often a struggle for people? Why do we find ourselves doing or saying things that aren't right? Understanding the answer to these questions and learning to establish character in our life starts with going back to how we were made in creation.

First, the order that the Creator set for us is *character before power.* When we return to character, we return to the natural state in which we were meant to function. We have seen that we were made in the image and likeness of God, and that one of God's first instructions to human beings was, "Be fruitful and increase in number; fill the earth and subdue it."[135] The whole world was to be filled with men, women, and children who manifested the nature of God as they exercised their unique purpose and gift. Accordingly, we should develop an environment conducive to demonstrating that nature. Internally, we should develop the mindset and qualities of character. Externally, we should create a community atmosphere that promotes and upholds ethical standards, such as integrity and justice.

While there is no such thing as an "ethical community," there is such a thing as a community of ethical people. Corporately, the people agree on the values by which they are going to live. That agreement is what creates a culture of morality. And that moral culture becomes the source of ethics for the community. An ethical culture always begins with individuals' personal commitment to live according to strong values.

Internally, we should develop the mindset and qualities of character. Externally, we should create a community atmosphere that promotes and upholds ethical standards, such as integrity and justice.

HOW HUMAN BEINGS LOST CHARACTER

A basic quality of the Creator's nature is that it doesn't change. We must therefore ask questions such as the following: "How did human beings as a race—made in God's image and likeness—lose the continual manifestation of His character?" "When did we stop being always consistent, always predictable, always trustworthy, always just, always merciful and compassionate, and so forth, as the Creator is?" "Why did we start to demonstrate unethical characteristics so that our world has veered so far away from being an expression of His nature?"

We talked earlier about how the first human beings rejected God's law. Let's briefly review that incident. Ironically, human beings lost their ability to consistently manifest the Creator's nature because the first man and woman heeded the false accusation that God wasn't treating them with true character—that He was not being just. When His trustworthiness was called into question, they made a decision to doubt His authenticity. Then, for the sake of gaining power for themselves, they broke a key law He had established for them.[136]

The principle that the first human beings violated had been designed to protect them so that they would not suffer the consequences of living outside of God's nature. In breaking this principle, they went against the very means that would have safeguarded them. Because they *chose* to live outside of God's nature, their character became warped. This indicates that, in some way, their character did not depend on nature alone—it also required an ongoing decision to remain in that nature. Today, we face the same type of decision: Will we live by our established principles, beliefs, values, moral standards, and ethical code? This is a choice we make on a daily basis.

The first humans' tragic decision caused humanity to suffer the consequences of a loss of God's true nature—including the onset of strife, sickness, and physical death. The fundamental source of all of humanity's deficiencies and problems was—and is—its rejection of the Creator's principles. This rejection is what the Scriptures call "sin." It is why human nature is described as being "fallen." Human nature once existed on a high ethical plane, but it descended into a place where it often manifests only a fraction of its former state.

RESULTS OF THE LOSS OF TRUE CHARACTER

Let's explore several results of humanity's rejection of the character and law of God.

DISTORTION OF THE CREATOR'S IMAGE

Because humanity lost God's true nature, it now has only a distorted image of that nature. The principal traits of fallen human beings are the opposite of genuine character: inconsistency, unpredictability, unfaithfulness, compromise, unjustness, prejudice, untrustworthiness, domination, vindictiveness, unforgiveness, cruelty, and so forth. All societies of the world suffer the symptoms of humanity's loss of character.

For example, there are people who connive to discredit their colleagues and other people in the workplace in order to get the promotions that these other individuals deserve. There are university students who cheat on tests in order to "achieve" a higher academic standing, with the result that they sometimes receive unfair advantages over others, such as higher-paying jobs. We wonder how these things can happen. (Some people aren't sure themselves why they commit some of these acts.) Moreover, humanity's warped character can cause the consciences of some people to be off-balance—they may lack a natural sense of guilt when doing wrong, or they may have an overactive conscience that causes them to feel continually feel guilty about things for which they are not responsible.

So, all human corruption stems from our loss of God's character as an intrinsic element of our own nature. Human beings are still capable of exercising moral conduct, but this involves making the continual decision to embrace strong convictions and values. And we are all inconsistent in this endeavor, because sound character is no longer natural to us.

CONFUSION ABOUT SELF-IMAGE AND SELF-WORTH

Another result of human beings' rejection of God's image is that they lost their own essence. They became confused about who they were, what they were born to be, and how they were to live. They no longer had a clear sense of purpose and meaning in the world. And they forfeited the feeling of acceptance and worth that comes from being in unbroken relationship with their Creator.

INSTABILITY

Without character, human beings also became unstable. This is why it is often hard for us to depend on others. Many people neglect to keep their promises. For example, on their wedding day, a couple gets dressed up, stands in front of a clergyperson or a justice of the peace, and makes promises to each other such as, "I will love and cherish you until I die!" Then, at some point after the honeymoon, the husband or wife may lose interest and leave—sometimes to run off with someone else. If your spouse has left you, you understand what I mean. You had a beautiful wedding in which everything was picture-perfect: the preacher, the gorgeous bridal gown and tailored tuxedo, the flowers, the rings, and more. It was an ideal day. And now you are wondering what happened to the marriage. Such heartbreak occurs because many people are unstable and inconsistent. They haven't made the conscious decision to establish strong values and truly commit to them.

If someone is unstable, it doesn't matter what they promise—you can't trust it. As the biblical writer James said, "Can both fresh water and salt water flow from the same spring? My brothers and sisters, can a fig tree bear olives, or a grapevine bear figs? Neither can a salt spring produce fresh water."[137] If the source hasn't changed, the result will be the same. James also wrote, "The one who doubts is like a wave of the sea, blown and tossed by the wind.... Such a person is double-minded and unstable in all they do."[138] An unstable person is like the waves of the sea—unpredictable, changeable.

That is why, when we meet people who have strong character, we admire and love them. It is because they are a picture of our original self. A person of character gives us a glimpse of what all human beings used to be like and what most of us, deep down, desire to be like. Let us become inspired to return to our true self—the image of God.

> *A person of character gives us a glimpse of what all human beings used to be like and what most of us, deep down, desire to be like.*

THE RESTORATION OF CHARACTER

Earlier, I described how the Creator's plans for human beings did not include allowing them to languish in a state in which they lacked His nature—and experienced all the resulting consequences. In His faithfulness and trustworthiness, He initiated a plan to restore humanity to Himself. This plan involved giving us a renewed nature, one by which we would again be able to share His character and consistently follow His life-giving principles.

He accomplished this plan through Jesus of Nazareth, also called Jesus Christ. God testified about Him, "This is my Son, whom I love; with him I am well pleased."[139] Jesus said, "I and the Father are one."[140] Jesus was God's Son because He came from God, He was one with God, and He fully manifested God's character on earth. One of Jesus's disciples wrote about Him:

> In the beginning was the Word, and the Word was with God, and the Word was God. He was with God in the beginning. Through him all things were made; without him nothing was made that has been made. In him was life, and that life was the light of all mankind.... The Word became flesh and made his dwelling among us. We have seen his glory, the glory of the one and only Son, who came from the Father, full of grace and truth.[141]

And Paul of Tarsus wrote, "For in Christ all the fullness of the Deity lives in bodily form."[142] Jesus had the same nature and Spirit as God. And His purpose for coming to the earth was to restore the image of God in us. The Scriptures are very clear that we need a new nature: "No one can enter the kingdom of God unless they are born of water and the Spirit."[143]

Therefore, Jesus came to give us back our character. No one can be restored to the Creator's nature except through Him.[144] Jesus Christ, as the Son of God, was the only One who could represent both the Creator and His created beings in order to fix the breach between the two and bring about full reconciliation and restoration.

When Jesus Christ died on the cross, He paid the price for our fallen human nature. He also paid the price for all the times when we ourselves have acted contrary to the character and laws of our Creator. When we acknowledge and accept what He did for us, we are restored to God and receive His nature within us once again. This enables us to experience a lasting transformation by which we can manifest His image and develop genuine character according to His principles. In this life, we can expect to experience a process of ongoing growth and maturation in the way we manifest the Creator's nature. God described His plan of restoration in this way: "I will put my law in their minds and write it on their hearts. I will be their God, and they will be my people."[145]

AGREEING WITH GOD

Remember that whenever we go against the Creator's law, it doesn't hurt God—His peace and integrity remain intact. However, it hurts us and shuts us down. After we are restored to God and receive His nature, what should we do if we once again violate one of His laws on the path to maturity? How do we get back on track so we can move forward and walk with character?

I grew up believing that when you confessed your sin, it meant that you were supposed to say what you did and tell God how sorry you were about it. However, when I was in college, I took a course in Hebrew. In one class, my professor, Dr. Hayden, was discussing the translation of various words, one of which was *confession*. I learned that the Hebrew word for confession doesn't really mean to bring up anything with God. Dr. Hayden explained it in this way: "The word confess means that you agree with God. If your heart condemns you, if the Lord says in your heart that what you did was wrong, you just agree it's wrong."

We often try to explain to God why we did something wrong and offer an excuse or justification for it, but this means we have not confessed in the sense of agreeing that it is wrong. We shouldn't try to explain it but simply say, "God, You are right. This is wrong. I have gone against Your law."

Another word we hear in relation to sin is *repent*. The acts of confession and repentance are distinct. To confess means to agree that something is wrong, while to repent means to go in the other direction. Thus, to repent means to change your mind about what you did, and to intend not to do it again. When we do this, we reopen access to the benefits of obedience to God's laws.

You may think, for example, that you're getting away with some private things God doesn't know about, but God knows everything. He sees what we're doing when no one else is watching. If you're secretly flirting with violating God's laws, He is giving you an opportunity to sort this thing out now because, eventually, it's going to harm you and the fulfillment of your purpose.

I want you to think carefully about this. Going against God's law can shut down the entire success principle. Whenever your conscience tells you that what you're doing is not right, just say, "God, You're right," and then immediately cease doing it. You can turn away from it. Whenever you do this, you reinforce character in your life.

In the next chapter, we will talk about how to intentionally establish values and standards for our life to build character.

18

ASSIMILATING PURPOSE, VALUES, AND VISION

"For where your treasure is, there your heart will be also."
—Jesus of Nazareth[146]

At the beginning of the previous chapter, I said that we shouldn't expect our success to carry us because, if we are not careful, we can misuse the power and influence that come with it, leading to ethical or moral failure. Therefore, instead of expecting our success to carry us, we need to let our success be carried by our character. Developing character will also enable us to cultivate enduring positive influence as we fulfill our purpose—a topic we will discuss more fully in the final section of this book.

Having good character is like having a personal security system for your life. Many people install security devices in their homes and places of business to protect them from thieves who would try to steal from them and from intruders who would try to harm their family members or employees. If someone were to try to open a window of a home or business that was electronically armed by a security system, an alarm would go off, exposing the intruder, with the goal of scaring them off, while alerting the security company. Or, suppose a trespasser intent on stealing or ransacking managed to sneak into an office building during working hours and lie low until everyone had left for the day? The building's security system, if installed properly, would detect their movement the moment they came out of hiding. The system would set off a signal, alerting security and/or law enforcement officials to their presence.

We can "install" character in our lives so that it will work like a security system. We do this by focusing on the Manufacturer's laws and principles and then developing values and standards that correspond to them. These values and standards will alert us to, and protect us from, the negative effects of various outside influences—such as life's pressures, difficulties, and temptations. Negative outside influences can threaten our success by invading our lives and stealing our willpower, common sense, and better judgment. Values and standards also safeguard us from internal "intruders"—our own human frailties that cause us to rationalize immoral behavior and take ethical shortcuts. A person of principle does not change their values and standards, no matter the circumstances.

> *Values and standards safeguard us from internal "intruders"—our own human frailties that cause us to rationalize immoral behavior and take ethical shortcuts.*

WHAT ARE VALUES?

To better understand the nature of values, let's look at two related definitions. Values are...

- *Ideas, principles, and qualities on which you personally place high worth.* A value is a belief—in something or someone—that you esteem, on its own merits. For instance, you may value the idea of giving charitable aid to families whose wage earner has been laid off from work, or you may value the principle of "equal justice under law" or the quality of courage.

- *Standards or ideals that determine your conduct or policy.* To use a simple example, suppose you own a diamond ring, and you know the market value of diamonds and want to protect your asset. The value you place on your diamond ring will both predict and affect your behavior toward it. If you truly value it as a possession, you will keep it clean and put it in a safe place when you're not wearing it. You may even check on it periodically to make sure it has not been lost or stolen.

DEVELOPING VALUES

Successful people adhere to a value system by which they consider options for conduct, make decisions, and take action. They are identified by the positive values that they consider worthy and by which they have determined to live. For positive values to make a difference in your life and your journey of success, you must embrace the following steps:

1. IDENTIFY YOUR VALUES

Carefully think through what you truly value and then express your values in writing. Your values are your philosophy of life. They determine how you intend to conduct yourself. They are your guides for living, doing business, relating to other people, and relating to life. You need to settle them in your heart and mind so that you will have standards to live by. You must clarify what you will and will not do.

Keep in mind that identifying and articulating your values is usually not accomplished in one sitting. It takes a thoughtful evaluation of your purpose, convictions, and vision for the future. And, as you increasingly come to understand your inherent purpose and gifts, you should refine the written statement of your values.

2. BELIEVE IN YOUR VALUES

Values are not ideals to which you give mere mental assent, because they are an indispensable part of your ability to live a life of purpose and character. Therefore, you should embrace values you can truly believe in and have confidence in—those you affirm and by which you desire to live.

3. RECEIVE YOUR VALUES

You must believe in your values to the point that you "receive" them. In other words, you internalize them so that they can become a vital part of who you are. You receive your values by reviewing them often, thinking about them, and affirming their place in your life. King Solomon said, "As [a person] thinks in his heart [subconscious mind], so is he."[147]

4. ADHERE TO YOUR VALUES

As a result of the preceding steps, a successful person *adheres to* their values. These values become their parameters, or framework, for living. They measure everything against those parameters. For example, if you ask them to take some action or to participate in a cause, they will evaluate whether doing so would be in alignment with their purpose and values. If not, they will decline to take action or to participate.

People of character do not relinquish their values in the face of pressure to disregard their beliefs. They don't change their values based on what they think other people want them to do. Because their values are based on their convictions, they are willing to lose money, promotion, and other advantages for the sake of those values.

There is an important distinction between compromising one's beliefs and making a concession on an opinion so that a group can come to a consensus. In those circumstances, we are not to be uncompromising for its own sake, or for the purpose of making life hard for another individual. However, when moral issues are clearly at stake, we must steadfastly hold on to our values and ethical code.

Many people can't handle disagreement, criticism, or opposition because they just want to be accepted. When others try to pressure us to back off from our values, we have to be able to say, "I can't be 'bought,'" or "I'm not going to compromise," or "I must publicly express my principles regarding this issue." When you look back on your life, as the saying goes, "You may not remember the things that you *fell* for, but you will remember what you *stood* for."

Thus, you must not only believe in and internalize your values but also put them into practice if they are to guide your life. Periodically take time to evaluate if you are living according to your stated values.

5. SHARE YOUR VALUES

You need to be able to share your values with others in any corporate entity of which you are a part—whether it is a family, a business, an organization, a nation, or another group. Remember that a personal vision can be fulfilled only in conjunction with other people's visions as you share a common purpose. Similarly, corporate values are effective only when they become the personal values of all the members. Every member of an organization needs to be in general agreement with the corporate values.

If you study the life of Jesus of Nazareth, you will notice that He kept restating His values to His disciples and to the crowds who came to hear Him speak—values concerning human life and human worth; values about what He considered of greatest significance.

Thus, if you are a leader who sets a corporate vision, you should remind people often of what is valuable to the community and what is valuable to you personally. These values should not be a secret to those who are involved. Values must not only be heard but also "seen"—in other words, demonstrated, especially by you.

CULTIVATING PERSONAL CHARACTER

Today, many people lack a framework for evaluating the suitability and consequences of their conduct and policies. Our framework of values becomes our measure not only of *whether* we will do something but also, if so, *how* we will conduct ourselves while doing it.

No matter what our values may be, they guide our behavior and our policies—both private and public. Here are some steps toward building a framework for personal character.

DEVELOP A SET OF STANDARDS

Our standards are derived from our values. After you have developed a written statement of your values, you should also write down your personal standards or principles for living. Writing down the ideas and behaviors on which you place high worth will help you to identify and clarify them. In addition, if your standards are recorded in written form, you can put them in an accessible place (such as a computer file or a folder in your desk) so that you can continually refer to them.

Here are some examples of written standards that reflect values:

- A married person who values the institution of marriage might translate that value into a written moral standard in this way: "I value the institution of marriage, so my corresponding personal moral standard, or principle for living, is that I will be faithful, and remain faithful, to my spouse."
- A businessperson who values honesty might translate that value into the following standard: "I esteem the quality of honesty; therefore, my corresponding moral conviction, or principle, is that I will always tell the truth to my customers and never overcharge them or bill them for services that were not performed," or "I will treat my employees justly by giving them fair wages and ensuring the safety of their work environment."
- An individual who values the benefits of a strong and healthy physical body might write the following standard: "I value having a strong body that will enable me to live longer, be more productive, and enjoy life better. My corresponding moral conviction, or principle, is that I will maintain a fit body by regularly eating healthy foods and exercising, and by not abusing alcohol, drugs, or other addictive substances."

As someone who has lived under the constant pressure of public scrutiny, let me tell you that no one else will set moral standards for you. You must set your own. And then you must be fixed and stable in relation to them.

> *Our framework of values becomes our measure not only of whether we will do something but also, if so, how we will conduct ourselves while doing it.*

INTEGRATE YOUR THOUGHTS, WORDS, AND ACTIONS

The words *integrate* and *integrity* are both derived from the Latin word *integer,* meaning "whole" and "entire." Thus, one definition of *integrate* is "to form, coordinate, or blend into a functioning or unified whole."[148] Having character means making a *continual* effort to integrate your thoughts, words, and actions. You should be able to declare, "What I say, what I do, and who I am are the same." Achieving such consistency takes daily discipline.

If we are to be people of principle, our private life and our public life must be ethically "one." This means we must be honest when no one else is watching us. When we say something in public, we must still mean what we said when we are in private. A person with integrity is the same person all the time, night or day, hot or cold, in good times or in bad. They believe what they say, and they say what they believe. They say what they do, and they do what they say. There is no dichotomy.

When we lack integrity, we are disingenuous, or "two-faced." Let's look at an illustration of this concept from the origins of the acting profession. The Greeks were the first to develop drama. While they started out using only a chorus of people to narrate a story, they later incorporated into that format an individual who could play five different parts, or characters, by wearing different masks, changing them according to the particular role they were playing.

Interestingly, the word the Greeks used for this person was *hypokrites,* from which we get the English word *hypocrite*. Similarly, the word *hypocrisy* comes from the Greek word *hypokrisis,* meaning "acting on the stage, pretense," from *hypokrinesthai,* meaning "play a part, pretend."[149] In its original form, "hypocrite" was not a negative term; it merely referred to the actors who wore masks on the stage while playing multiple parts. However, the term evolved into the idea of a person of "many faces"—someone whose real identity was not what it appeared to be.

It is wearying to pretend to be someone you're not. It's as if you have more than one person living inside of you working at cross-purposes. Character is who you are—reputation is the mask.

We must ask ourselves, "Am I manifesting who I really am in my interactions with others?" That can be a tough question to ask yourself—and to answer—but it is a necessary one. We have to start taking off our masks so that who we really are can be seen. Then, we must work to develop our character so that other people will be able to fully trust what we say and do.

MAKE SACRIFICES IN SUPPORT OF YOUR PRINCIPLES

A person of principle possesses beliefs so strong that they are willing to sacrifice for them—to experience the loss of popularity, friendships, colleagues, financial gain, and success for their sake. I believe such a quality must be reintroduced in our society by individuals of genuine principle.

Mahatma Gandhi made some major sacrifices for his vision. For instance, he went on several hunger strikes, one of which drew attention to the unjust treatment of India's poorest classes in the caste system, the "untouchables." People will continue to remember Gandhi for generations because of his willingness to sacrifice for what he believed in.

IMPOSE SELF-DISCIPLINE IN KEEPING WITH YOUR VALUES AND STANDARDS

In conjunction with making sacrifices, we must impose daily discipline upon ourselves so that we will remain aligned with our convictions and continue to adhere to our principles. Discipline begins with our mind. Again, it involves setting priorities for ourselves that determine our choices and direct our behavior. The key to being disciplined is to set parameters for your life in relation to both your moral standards and your daily activities—what you will and will not accept for yourself, and what you will and will not participate in. We are self-disciplined when we understand that there are purposes and goals in life that are immeasurably greater than temporary pleasures, secondary objectives, and everyday distractions.

When someone pursues their vision without having established values, they are attempting to reach their destiny without the necessary component of discipline. For example, regardless of how great a person's dream might be—whether it is to build a family, a church, a business, or a country—the entire process must be balanced by clear, strong values that guide their conduct. As we have seen, if you don't have discipline, you will short-circuit your destiny and be in danger of losing it completely.

An important principle to remember is that there's no "break" in life from character. There is no point at which we will have "arrived" so that we no longer have to concern ourselves with values and principles. We must therefore keep vigil over our character. For instance, it is very easy to be tempted to lie. Suppose you were laid off from your job, and you found some short-term work through a temporary agency. Then, at a social function, you meet a wealthy business executive who asks you, "So, what do you do for a living?" You don't want to seem inferior, so you inflate your job description. Character requires daily maintenance because, every day—and often many times throughout the day—our character will be tested.

If you endeavor to do what is right, I guarantee that you will eventually emerge at the top. Don't worry about people who take shortcuts or compromise to get ahead. Don't be jealous of them. They will ultimately fail.

VISION AND VALUES

Let's conclude this chapter by further exploring the relationship between vision and values. I often say, "Leaders stand *for* something—vision. Leaders stand *on* something—values." This statement is true for anyone pursuing their purpose because everyone is a leader in their own gifting and domain. And, of these two elements, values are of higher importance than vision. If we don't have an active commitment to our values, moral standards, principles, discipline, and ethical code, all of our endeavors will be weakened—and may even be nullified.

VISION IS AN INTERPRETATION OF VALUES

Your vision should interpret your values in the sense that it should reflect and communicate them. Earlier in this book, we talked about how someone might discover their gift by recognizing that they are angry about the fact that young people are living on the streets without any sense of purpose. That person's vision might be to help young people who are members of gangs that are undermining their community to become engaged in positive activities that will build up the community instead. This vision communicates that the individual values the lives of young people and that they value improving the quality of life in their community.

Similarly, an organization's vision reflects its corporate values. For instance, suppose the vision of a home-based business was to create exquisitely embroidered garments to sell to specialty stores, the proceeds of which would supplement the family's income. This vision communicates that that the business, through its owner, values creativity, quality, enterprise, and financial stability.

Therefore, when leaders in politics, religion, education, business, economics, sports, and other fields invest their time and money in a vision, that vision can be used as a measure for assessing their principal values. As Jesus of Nazareth said, "For where your treasure is, there your heart will be also."

VALUES ATTRACT SIMILAR VALUES

It is generally the case that people who hold particular values are drawn to other people who hold the same values. Applying this point to personal relationships, we know that friendships are forged among people who have similar interests and preferences.

My close friends and associates share my values. As I expressed previously, there are other people with whom I am unable to associate. My experiences with them have revealed that they don't value the things I value; in fact, sometimes they value things that I believe are detrimental. That doesn't mean that I intentionally snub them. Yet, as a leader, I have to protect my character, and a close tie with them would not only be ethically unhealthy for me, but it might also give the impression to others that I support their values.

Values are so important that they should be the basis of our key associations. The same point applies to corporate relationships—for example, companies doing business with one another and governments making agreements and treaties with other countries and supporting various international causes. When considering an association, we should ask ourselves, "What overt or underlying values are involved in this decision? What binding alliances am I making?"

VISION IS PROTECTED BY VALUES

Your vision is only as safe as the values that undergird it. If you cherish a great vision but don't value the principles that would enable you to realize it, you may as well not pursue that vision. There needs to be a marriage of purpose and principles. You have to *know* your purpose, but you must *live by* your principles. In this sense, vision may be compared to the head, and values to the heart. We should take the advice of an ancient proverb that says, "Above all else, guard your heart, for everything you do flows from it."[150]

It has been said that "the process is as important as the product," and this is certainly true in regard to fulfilling one's vision. Years ago, my organization decided to construct a large building called the Diplomat Center. I envisioned how it would be used to teach people about their purpose as leaders. So, I was excited about it, and I was caught up with securing the property, raising the money, and working long hours to see it come to fruition. However, one day, I sensed that God was saying to me, "I am not pleased with you." I was confused, so I asked, "What are You talking about? I'm doing Your will. You told me to build the building." He said, "You're not leading the people. You are driving them." It broke my heart to realize that I had been driving the people who were involved in the vision, rather than inspiring them.

Then, I felt God saying, "You have passion, and passion is good, but you have no *com*passion. Stop everything. I want you to get your balance back." Deeply convicted, I went into a brief season of solitude in order to regain the balance between my passion and my compassion. The people in my organization were supposed to love this project, not just endure it. So, after reflecting on the situation, I had to go to the people and publicly ask them to forgive me for breaking the law of compassion. I explained to them that, from that point on, we would work together. My confession changed the whole spirit of the organization. People donated more money toward the project, and they also dedicated their time and their skills to see it accomplished.

The ethical issue I had to deal with was that I had been standing *for* something—the idea of how the new building would support the organization's vision—but I hadn't been standing *on* the values that were needed for the process of carrying it out. Again, having character requires more than discovering what you were born to do and pursuing the fulfillment of your vision; it involves pursuing the fulfillment of your vision in a way that corresponds with ethical principles.

This is why individual leaders and organizations alike should protect themselves against ethical breaches by setting strong values for themselves. An organization's governing board should decide what types of policies it will and will not sanction. A business should determine what standards it will not compromise on. A family should decide what media content it will and will not allow into the home. A corporate entity that has not established values for itself lacks moral protection. It is like a city without walls from ancient times that has left itself vulnerable to deadly attack by enemy armies.

One of my close friends is a distinguished gentleman named Dr. Richard Demeritte Jr. He and I met years ago when he was the ambassador to England from the Bahamas. He has also served as the ambassador to the European Union. Once, when we were talking together, he told me a time-honored value that his father had conveyed to him: "When in doubt, do what's right." This statement provides extremely valuable yet easy-to-remember ethical advice. When you are faced with a moral choice, just do what's right! A person of character should always live in that way.

PART FIVE

THE INFLUENCE OF SUCCESS

19

SUCCESS LEADS TO INFLUENCE

"Try not to become a man of success but rather try to become a man of value. He is considered successful in our day who gets more out of life than he puts in. But a man of value will give more than he receives."
—Albert Einstein[151]

One of the reasons we focus on success is because success naturally brings us influence with other people. Just as we were born to be a success in a domain of life, we were born to be an influence in that domain—and even beyond. On the journey of success, you will develop into a person who inspires and impacts others. You were meant to influence your family, community, business, government, and more in beneficial ways.

PREREQUISITES OF INFLUENCE

BEING SUCCESSFUL

Many people don't put forth any influence, and, for this reason, they are unduly influenced by other people. As I wrote earlier, if we don't have a sense of our personal purpose and gifting, other people will control our future and destiny. They will make decisions for us, dictating what kind of life we will have and, in this sense, controlling our worth. What a tragedy. In contrast, those who discover and understand who they are and what their life's purpose is will influence their environments more than their environments influence them.

You will never have influence until you are successful, and you will never be successful until you have influence. The two are connected. Once again, our goal should be to focus on fulfilling our purpose, which will lead to our becoming successful in the arena of our gifting. Then, when our success gives us influence, we are to use that influence for good in a variety of ways as our success increases.

Consider the example of Jesus of Nazareth. He became successful before He was influential. Jesus grew up in a little village. Archeologists have excavated the area where the original town of Nazareth stood. Based on the results of this excavation work, Nazareth has been described as "an out-of-the-way hamlet of around 50 houses on a patch of about four acres.... It was evidently populated by Jews of modest means."[152] Nazareth was really a small settlement—humble and without much influence in the surrounding world.

When Nathanael, who became one of Jesus's disciples, initially heard that Jesus was from that small town, he said, "Nazareth! Can anything good come from there?"[153] Later, when Jesus was living in the town of Capernaum, people said, "Is this not Jesus, the son of Joseph, whose father and mother we know? How can he now say, 'I came down from heaven'?"[154] In essence, they were saying, "Who do You think You are?" They were focused only on the hometown and family from which Jesus came; they didn't understand His purpose, which transcended those elements.

When Jesus was about to begin His ministry, He knew that if He were to fulfill His purpose, He had to succeed at something, which would give Him influence. So what did He do? He went looking for a problem, and He found one. As I wrote earlier, success often begins with our identifying a problem to solve. What was the problem Jesus found? It was three young fishermen sitting on the beach with an empty boat. These men were professionals, but they hadn't caught any fish, and they didn't know what to do about it. So Jesus addressed their problem using one of His gifts.

What was that gift? It was the gift of exercising dominion over the earth. He told the fishermen to go back out onto the water and try again. This time, they caught so many fish that their boats were in danger of sinking. He had solved their problem. What happened after that? "They pulled their boats up on shore, left everything and followed him."[155] That's influence.

On another occasion, Jesus used His dominion gift once more to calm a raging storm at sea. After this, His disciples (including the fishermen whose problem He had solved earlier) said to Him, "What kind of man is this? Even the winds and the waves obey him!"[156] In other words, Jesus had distinguished Himself from other men. People had thought that He was a normal man until He started exercising His gifts. This is another example of how success begins with being distinct from other people. Immediately, Jesus became a celebrity—He was celebrated. No wonder the fishermen were willing to drop their nets, leave their fishing business, and join Him.

Jesus became successful by exercising His gifts in various ways, making Him influential. Suddenly, people were listening to Him. Large crowds began to seek Him out. Many people even got to the point where they said, "We will follow You." Your influence is manifested when other people change their priorities for your priorities. In this sense, influence can be defined as the capacity to cause other people to listen to you or to follow you. When you exercise your gift, people will ask, "What manner of person are you? You solved a problem that we couldn't solve. You used a gift we didn't know you had."

Influence can be defined as the capacity to cause other people to listen to you or to follow you.

In another example, David was an unknown shepherd boy without any influence in the world, yet he became influential throughout the entire nation of Israel. How? He succeeded in solving a problem that the nation couldn't solve. He killed the giant who was threatening Israel's army and, therefore, endangering the whole country. A young boy killed a giant and, in one day, become a national hero, automatically becoming prominent.[157] Eventually, David became the king of his nation. That's influence.

HAVING WEALTH AND WISDOM

Thus, success, in itself, is a major key to having influence. A second key, which is related to the first, is wealth, or prosperity. Wealthy people have influence. If we fail, people are much less likely to listen to us (though trial and error and setbacks can be part of the process of success). If we're broke, people don't usually look to us as an example or seek to talk with us.

There is nothing wrong with gaining wealth, in itself, even though, as I indicated earlier, many people have been taught to think that there is. The problem is not wealth but rather how some people go about gaining it and the attitude that they have toward it. That's why I prefer to define wealth by giving it a criterion: honest wealth. Honest wealth makes you influential.

Recall that Moses made this statement to the people whom he led: "Remember the LORD your God, for it is he who gives you the ability to produce wealth."[158] It is important to note that the biblical exhortations concerning money, including Paul of Tarsus's statement "The love of money is a root of all kinds of evil,"[159] do not warn against possessing money or wealth but rather against allowing money or wealth to possess us. Loving money at the expense of the dignity, value, and welfare of others is an abuse of our ability to obtain wealth. Power, authority, position, money, and so forth are meant to be tools that enable us to achieve a noble purpose—not to serve selfish or dishonorable ends.

According to the first book written by Moses, God told Abraham, the father of the Israelites, in effect, "I'm going to bless you and make you a blessing." Abraham became the richest man in his region. Why would God want to make him rich? In order to give him influence. Abraham was very comfortable with the power that he had. He was not proud in relation to it, but he was grateful for it and handled it responsibly. He had influence with others, and he credited that influence to God.[160]

We can see that there are different ways to become influential. David's son King Solomon never killed a giant. As a matter of fact, there's no record in the Bible of Solomon ever going to war. He was not a fighter, but Solomon inherited wealth and increased in riches. He also had a gift that drew people to him: extraordinary wisdom.

Solomon became the most influential king in the history of Israel, and other rulers of the earth traveled from afar to have an audience with him. One of them was the queen of Sheba. She had heard about Solomon's wealth and wisdom and came to see them for herself. I believe that wisdom and wealth always go together. I think that's why Solomon did not ask God for wealth. He asked God for wisdom, which will always attract wealth.[161]

Our scope of influence is really based on the level of success that we have. LeBron James is one of the top basketball players in the world. He was simply a young man from Akron, Ohio, raised by a single mother struggling to make ends meet, but his success in sports makes him celebrated. A celebrity is someone whom a majority of the people celebrate, and therefore they consider that individual to be a person of influence. LeBron James's success as a professional on the basketball court gives him influence in many other areas of life as well. There is an important principle in this: if we become successful and influential in one area, we often become influential in other areas as well.

We must therefore always consider the aspect of influence whenever we discuss success. And just as we have learned not to "try" to be successful—because success is a natural byproduct of exercising our gifting and applying the laws and principles of life—we shouldn't "try" to be influential. We can't decide one day, "I'm going to be an influence on others." It doesn't work that way. Again, we need to focus on pursuing our gift in our domain while following God's principles and asking Him to give us wisdom for gaining wealth. As we do this, we will naturally gain and exert influence.

THE NATURE OF INFLUENCE

To better understand the nature of influence, it is helpful to look at some additional definitions of this concept. The general idea we previously noted was, "Influence is the capacity to cause other people to listen to you or to follow you." Let's dig deeper into this idea.

THE DIFFERENCE BETWEEN INFLUENCE AND DOMINATION

When you think about it, all of us already exercise some influence—whether positive or negative. When you have a child of your own to raise, you exert influence. When you know more about a particular subject than others do and are in a position to teach it to them, you exert influence. When you are placed in a position of responsibility over your peers, you exert influence. Moreover, all people naturally want to influence the world around them. Everyone is in the influence game in one way or another—whether it's a salesperson trying to influence a prospective client, a child trying to influence a parent, or a young man trying to influence a young woman.

Everyone desires influence; however, we've often confused influence with domination. There are many people, past and present, who have swayed others using threats and violence, but we don't call that true influence. We call it manipulation, oppression, or dictatorship. Nero, Hitler, and Idi Amin were all influential. They exerted their wills over people, but they were not leaders in the true sense. Leadership influence is a powerful instrument, and we must always be aware of its potential to bring either good or harm to others.

According to the Creator's original design, we're not supposed to dominate other people—we're supposed to have dominion *over the earth* and its resources. If we don't understand this distinction, we will manipulate and abuse others and frustrate the expression of their own God-given purpose and gift. The true nature of success is for other people to be attracted to our gift, which is deployed in their service. So, exerting proper influence means inspiring others through the gift that we have been given.

Again, when you find your unique gift or special talent and commit to serving it to humanity, then your significance will cause people to seek you out. You will become an influence through exercising your gift rather than through manipulation. And, as I indicated in a previous chapter, the more you become a person whose gift is valued, the greater your influence will be.

I was invited to Las Vegas to speak to a group of twelve people who, combined, control over $100 billion. That day, I was their teacher from 8:00 a.m. until 4:00 p.m. This is the type of person I am influencing just from pursuing my purpose and exercising my gift. You, too, can have great influence if you follow the laws and principles that I have learned and have outlined in this book—again, not solely for your own sake but for the sake of serving your gift to the world. As I said earlier, a tree that bears fruit does not eat its own harvest; that harvest is meant to be shared for the good of others.

WHAT IS INFLUENCE?

For over thirty years, I have dedicated myself to the study of the subject of leadership. After thousands of hours of study, research, and reading hundreds of books on the subject, I determined to develop my own comprehensive definition of leadership as I have come to understand it. This definition incorporates the principal ingredients and components that I believe give birth to and sustain true leadership. It can be applied by anyone who desires to discover and release the gift within them, with its corresponding leadership potential:

> Leadership is the capacity to *influence* others through *inspiration* motivated by a *passion,* generated by a *vision,* produced by a *conviction,* ignited by a *purpose.*

The best way to approach this definition and appreciate its practical application is to start the process at the end of the statement. As you might have guessed, the process begins with an individual's discovery of a personal purpose that, when captured, ignites a conviction. This conviction generates a vision in the person's heart that stirs a passion. The force of this person's passionate pursuit of their vision inspires others who are stirred to participate in and cooperate with the vision. This ultimate effect is called "influence."

The purest form of leadership is influence through inspiration. I think of inspiration as the divine deposit of destiny in the heart of a person. If inspiration is the key to influence and thus the source of leadership, how do we inspire others? What is the source of inspiration? Simply put, the source of inspiration is *passion.* This component is the heart of influence and generates our energy and resilience. As I mentioned earlier, passion is birthed from a revelation of where we are headed in life. When a person discovers a sense of purpose, it produces a passion for pursuing it, and that passion is what inspires other people to want to join in the pursuit. Then, as people are inspired, their thinking and their lives are naturally influenced. Inspiration is an invitation to pursue something that is higher and better than we have had before—changing the status quo, creating something new, finding a solution to a problem, and so forth—and, in the process, to gain a sense of meaning and significance for our life.

Those who exercise positive influence don't try to prove themselves to others. They are more concerned with "manifesting" themselves, or revealing the purpose they were born to fulfill. To sum up, the essence of leadership influence is the ability to motivate other people to take action and effect change, and you can't influence if you don't inspire. You can't inspire if you don't have passion, and you won't have passion unless you are convinced about your purpose, convictions, and vision.

> *Inspiration is an invitation to pursue something that is higher and better than we have had before—changing the status quo, creating something new, finding a solution to a problem—and, in the process, to gain a sense of meaning and significance for our life.*

THE IMPACT OF INFLUENCE

The influence we exert can impact the lives of other people in significant ways. Let's take a look at some of those ways.

MINDSET

Through influence, we can transform people's outlook to the point where their perspective becomes completely different from the way they formerly thought. For example, someone might use rhetorical skills to convince people that what they believed was good is actually evil, and vice versa—altering their values and conduct. Such influence is a tremendous power that we need to acknowledge and discipline in our own life, ensuring that we do not abuse it—especially since a change in mindset almost always leads to a change in behavior.

In Shakespeare's play *Julius Caesar,* after Brutus and his fellow conspirators kill Caesar, believing him to be a tyrant, the character of Mark Antony uses his communication skills to turn the crowd from an admiration for Brutus to a seething desire to kill him and his accomplices. We must always weigh the consequences of what we hear and receive from others, including our leaders.

In contrast, an enlightened perspective is a gift that we can give to other people. For example, when Harriet Beecher Stowe wrote the novel *Uncle Tom's Cabin,* she changed the mindset of tens of thousands of people who had been either neutral toward the institution of slavery in America or accepting of it. By putting a personal face on the issue, she showed that slaves were people rather than "property," so that many citizens began to support efforts to abolish slavery.

CHARACTERISTICS AND ATTITUDES

Someone in a position of influence who lacks conviction can transfer their complacency or timidity to those who follow them. There is an account in one of the books of Moses in which Moses sent twelve spies to scope out the promised land and its inhabitants to prepare the nation of Israel to enter it. When the spies returned, ten of them expressed their fear of the inhabitants, declaring that they could never defeat them: "We seemed like grasshoppers in our own eyes, and we looked the same to them."[162] Two of the spies insisted they would still be victorious, but the people grumbled and took on the perspective of the ten who were afraid and felt like "grasshoppers" in their own eyes. As a result, the victory was delayed for forty years—almost two generations. The people lost out, largely because they allowed themselves to be influenced by the fearful mindset of others.

In contrast, when someone holds deep convictions, they can transfer those convictions to other people. For instance, they can rouse the fearful so that they will take bold and necessary action in the midst of a crisis. Winston Churchill, through his powerful speeches, stirred the English people to continue standing against Nazi Germany after the fall of France.

In one of these speeches, he famously declared, "The Battle of France is over. I expect that the Battle of Britain is about to begin.... Let us therefore brace ourselves to our duties, and so bear ourselves that, if the British Empire and its Commonwealth last for a thousand years, men will still say, '*This* was their finest hour.'"[163] Churchill influenced the citizens of his nation to maintain courage and resilience under circumstances of extreme testing.

MORALITY

The ethics of someone with influence can sway those who admire and/or follow them. This can occur through people either accepting the corporate values and policies that the individual encourages as a leader of a group or organization or imitating (or accepting) their behavior. If a leader is a high-ranking official over a nation, the leader's morals can permeate an entire culture. You may come from a country where the leaders have tremendous gifts, communicate well, and are competent in various leadership techniques—but are lacking in ethical convictions. Many leaders do not take responsibility for their actions. They feel they should experience no consequences when they betray the trust of their constituents—whether their employees, their families, or the public. Such attitudes and behaviors do not go unnoticed by followers, so that many people may begin to think, "He's a leader, and he did such and such and got away with it, so I can do it, too."

This is why it is essential for people who are in positions of influence to recognize and assess the values they currently hold and to establish or reestablish ethical principles that they will commit themselves to stand upon, such as we discussed in the previous section of this book.

COMMITMENT

As we noted, when someone has strong convictions about something, their passion for it will become contagious among other people who then commit to the person's vision. An individual's commitment can be transferred to enough people that their personal conviction eventually becomes a national movement. Their principles can initiate an irresistible process of reform. Martin Luther King Jr.'s vision gave him a passion that inspired and influenced "average" people—such as housewives, carpenters, masons, teachers, and religious leaders—to march in nonviolent protest against the refusal of certain states within the US to acknowledge and permit voting rights for Blacks. A number of them personally faced the resistance of policemen armed with clubs, dogs, water hoses, and tear gas. Why would anyone willingly risk being beaten with a billy club or choked by tear gas? What kind of man would influence people to actually do that? Someone with genuine commitment and conviction.

If you try to avoid an issue or a consequence, people won't follow you. But if you meet it squarely and remain constant in your convictions, others will join you.

DESTINY

A person of influence who lacks character can condemn those who follow them to an appalling fate. In the 1970s, cult leader Jim Jones convinced people to leave loved ones and live with him in the jungles of Guyana. Several years later, he led 909 of his followers to their deaths by inducing them to drink cyanide—then he shot himself to death.

In contrast, the influence of someone who holds convictions can lead people to a positive destiny they might not otherwise have reached. Czech playwright and dissident Václav Havel, who had long decried the dehumanizing elements of communism, helped precipitate the nonviolent Velvet Revolution in Czechoslovakia in 1989 that effectively led to the end of communist rule there. Havel and other dissidents formed the Civic Forum to plan the dismantlement of communism in their country. Timothy Garton Ash, a historian who witnessed the forum, said, "It was extraordinary the degree to which everything ultimately revolved around this one man.... In almost all the forum's major decisions and statements, he was the final arbiter, the one person who could somehow balance the very different tendencies and interests in the movement."[164] Havel became the last president of Czechoslovakia and the first president of a new Czech Republic.

Thus, the impact of influence can be varied and pervasive. In chapter 20, we will explore how you can use the influence that comes from success in an inspirational and honorable way to bring positive change in the world.

20

TRANSFORMATION THROUGH INFLUENCE

"The happiest individuals are those who do the most to make others useful and happy."
—Booker T. Washington[165]

One of my goals in writing about success and influence is to encourage you to be willing to become part of the answer to the challenges facing your community and nation. My desire is that you would go into the world and contribute to its transformation, duplicating in the lives of others what you have learned about how to discover inherent purpose and gifting and how to live according to the laws and principles of life. It is easy for us to criticize and complain about the state of the world. Let our days of complaining end so that we can become a solution to the problems we face, working to correct what is wrong.

Many nations in the world are struggling, and our world systems are in flux and in dire need of help. Across the globe, we have seen turbulent changes such as the following: Political confusion. Economic crisis.

Ideological reinvention. Philosophical confusion. Moral manipulation. Values vacillation. Religious conflict. International terrorism. Failed states. The fall and disgrace of political, civic, and religious leaders. This is the kind of world we live in. We have to learn to adapt to these changes but not to adopt them.

When we consider the condition of the world and the many needs people have, we must remember that whatever we allow, we cannot criticize. Whatever we avoid, we cannot change. Whatever we permit, we are responsible for. If we don't become involved in addressing the needs around us, we have to keep quiet about them.

Let us be people of initiative. To take initiative, we must study, think about, and discern the environment in which we live, discovering how to effectively apply the Creator's life-giving principles to it. If you have been praying about the world situation, you must become part of the answer to your own prayer.

TRANSFORMING THE ENVIRONMENT

God's number one passion is to manifest the influence of the kingdom of heaven and its culture on earth. Culture has to do with the setting in which something develops. To culture something means to grow something in a created environment.[166] God's plan is to create the environment of heaven on earth within which everything on earth is meant to grow. That is why the first word that the Creator used for Adam's environment was the word *Eden*: "Now the LORD God had planted a garden in the east, in Eden; and there he put the man he had formed."[167]

In my view, Eden is not a place. God "planted a garden." That doesn't mean God planted trees. The Hebrew word translated as "planted" can also mean "established." So, *planted* suggests something that is organized, and *garden* indicates structure or order.[168] God created an environment of order and then put human beings in it. He told them, in essence, "Multiply this all over the planet until the whole earth becomes like this spot, this environment."[169]

Someone has said, "If you want something in your life you've never had, you'll have to do something you've never done."[170] To participate in transformation, you have to take a leap and leave behind those who don't want to change the world, those who just want to remain in a safe place for themselves. You have to go to the unknown territory of *influence.*

> *To participate in transformation, you have to take a leap and leave behind those who don't want to change the world, those who just want to remain in a safe place for themselves.*

INFLUENCE, NOT IMPOSITION

How do we go about making a difference in our environment? The first thing we must realize is that the world I described above cannot heal itself because the solution to the earth's problems is not found on earth. Those who have a solution from another place—God's kingdom, with its laws and principles—are valuable. That makes you valuable because you have reconnected to the other place. You have access to resources that many people on earth don't have.

In the midst of the world's upheaval, our goal, again, is influence—not domination or imposition. The culture of God's nature does not correspond with the destructive ideas that have developed from fallen human nature, and such ideas are dominating our nations today. It will take people of principle to bring about transformation and not merely become absorbed into the existing system.

Once more, you were born not just to make a living but to make a *difference.* If you get involved in making a difference, God will ensure that you make a living. So, start working for change in your environment. Become active. Let your success be a vehicle by which you become an influence for good in the world around you.

PRINCIPLES OF INFLUENCE

As you live out the laws of success and grow in influence, keep these principles in mind in order to effectively gain, exercise, and retain your influence:

EMPLOY THE LANGUAGE OF YOUR DOMAIN

We might also call this point "Speak People's Language." Whatever the domain of your gifting, that's the place you're supposed to begin exercising a positive influence. And this means that you have to know the language of that particular environment and identify with its interests. Every field of endeavor or profession—such as law, politics, business, manufacturing, education, medicine, entertainment, and technology—has its own language. You can't just go into any field and expect to succeed and be an influence in it if you aren't familiar with its language.

I keep studying the language of as many arenas as possible because I know I might find myself interacting with people in that environment. I use as my example Paul of Tarsus, who said, "I have become all things to all people so that by all possible means I might save some."[171] He learned people's language and culture so he could relate to them, and they to him. If you read the teachings of Jesus, you might be amazed at how much He talks about birds, seeds, trees, fields, flowers, snakes, sheep, and so on. Why did He do this? Because the original audience to whom He was speaking lived in a farming culture. He spoke their language.

Thus, to help bring about change through positive influence, you must convey the message of God's kingdom, with its laws and principles of success, to those who are in your field or in whatever realm of life in which you are operating. However, you should communicate in a way that people can relate to and understand by using examples from their domain, as well as from everyday life and the experience of the wider world.

USE WISDOM

Solomon wrote, "The fruit of the righteous is a tree of life, and the one who is wise saves lives."[172] Again, to be righteous simply means being aligned with God's laws. The Scriptures call Jesus "the wisdom *of* God" and "wisdom *from* God."[173] They doesn't specifically say that Jesus "has" wisdom. God has wisdom, and Jesus Christ is the wisdom of God in action. In what way did God send Jesus into the earth to save the world? Wisely, through relatable influence. God is described in the Scriptures as the almighty, omnipotent One. Paul of Tarsus called God "the blessed and only Ruler, the King of kings and Lord of lords, who alone is immortal and who lives in unapproachable light, whom no one has seen or can see."[174] This powerful, awesome God became a man to live among human beings, whom He had created. John, one of Jesus's closest disciples, wrote, "The Word became flesh and made his dwelling among us. We have seen his glory, the glory of the one and only Son, who came from the Father, full of grace and truth."[175] In other words, with Jesus, we are able to look upon the glory of God and not be afraid. God knew that in order to win people, He couldn't send someone whom people would be afraid of. His plan was, in effect, "I'm going to become just like them. They won't even recognize who I am until I've had an opportunity to show them My nature and teach them the laws and principles of My kingdom through influence."

For example, one time, Jesus met a woman at a well and asked her for water. His approachable influence in that conversation was so effective that they ended up talking about deep matters that related to connecting with the Creator; this impacted not only the woman but her whole community as well.[176] When you interact with other people, no matter how right you may think you are, it needs to be with influence, not forcefulness; wisdom, not volume. Remember that Solomon said, "The one who is wise saves lives."

Jesus told His disciples, "I send you out as sheep in the midst of wolves. Therefore be wise as serpents and harmless as doves."[177] There's that word *wise* again. I want you to understand the dynamics, the wisdom, of influence. Although you may experience "cultural clashes" with others as you live according to the Creator's principles and seek to share them, don't let those encounters cause you to respond in anger or fear toward other people. Use wisdom, and be patient. When you pursue your distinct purpose, attaining success and becoming a positive influence, you will fulfill your part in the purposes of God for the earth.

CONVINCE RATHER THAN OFFEND

This is an area in which we need to exercise wisdom. We won't influence people who are irritated to be around us! This applies to personal relationships, to business, to public service—every realm of life. It's not about how loud or direct you are. The goal is to persuade people, rather than offend them, by focusing on and communicating sound, life-giving principles.

For example, someone who has an unhealthy habit doesn't need you to tell them that they're doing something wrong. They likely know it already. They need hope for change, and you can bring that hope through influence.

We must take care in our interactions because once we offend someone, it's difficult to regain their trust. Solomon wrote, "A brother offended is harder to win than a strong city, and contentions are like the bars of a castle."[178] The term "strong city" refers to a city with walls around it. The result of offense is contention. People who are offended will fight with you, argue with you, test you, and resist you. So, seek to build people up.

FOCUS ON KINGDOM VALUES, NOT TRADITIONS

Earlier in this book, we talked about the difference between laws and rules, and how rules are man-made traditions that restrict people rather than guide them and give them freedom. Consider the ways in which you are interacting with people and carefully consider how you might be promoting mere tradition or rules rather than liberating laws and principles. You must learn the difference. Many people don't want to hear about tradition. They want to hear about principles that work, precepts that are valid. They want to know values and standards that are beneficial for them.

IMPACT RATHER THAN IMPOSE

Similarly, the goal of influence is impact rather than imposition. My wife and I traveled to a country where I had been invited to speak on leadership principles. In that country, it is illegal to talk about one's belief in Jesus. If you do, they will put you in jail. The people who had invited me asked me to speak to judges who served in the courts. (Those are the people who have the power to put you in jail!) They told me they wanted me to do a full-day seminar with these judges. So, I went into a hotel meeting room full of judges and talked to them about leadership.

After that, our hosts took us to a manufacturing plant where electronic products were made, and they said to me, "There are two thousand workers here. We want you to train them, as well as fifty or sixty managers, and then talk to the president of the company. You cannot mention God or

Jesus." I said, "Give me the microphone." When I was finished, they invited me back. After every session, people bought all my books—books that, incidentally, had references to God and Jesus in them. We were sold out.

Now, they had told me I couldn't talk about Jesus, and I spoke for hours and never quoted a single passage from the Bible. I just spoke their language and emphasized the Creator's laws and principles. I talked to them about business and economics and science. I spoke about management and investment. I spoke about leadership, and the sessions were powerful. They kept saying to me, "Where did you learn this?" or "This is amazing information you have." In reply, I would say something like, "I had a young Rabbi as a mentor."

After I returned home, I started receiving emails from people who had heard my talks and bought my books and who had connected with God and with Jesus. I didn't impose my beliefs on them. My beliefs came out in my principles, and then the people made their own decision about them. That is influence without imposition or domination.

FOCUS ON REASONS

As you talk with others, listen to their reasons for thinking and acting in the way they do. Every human being on earth has a reason why they believe what they believe. If you ignore their reason, they will not listen to you, and they may even reject you. If you want to communicate the laws of creation, and someone says, "I'm an atheist," don't ignore that. There's a reason why they don't believe in God and that they believe what they believe. You can ask them, "Why are you an atheist?" and "What's the reason you came to this conclusion?"

Their answer may blow your mind. We have no idea what some people have been through. I talked with one man who, when he was a boy, was told by his mother that God loved them both. Then, when he was only seven, his mother was raped and killed in front of him. The man said, "I told God, 'Go to he--.' There's no God. God didn't save my mother."

After I heard this, I said, "I see why you don't believe in God. I understand." All of a sudden, he liked me, and we became friends. We maintained a friendship, and, two years later, he reconnected with God and Jesus.

So, whenever you talk with someone who has a different opinion than you do or doesn't think like you do, don't ignore or reject them but ask them why they think they way they do, and try to understand their viewpoint. That's how you influence people for good.

MAKE FRIENDS, NOT "CONVERTS"

Jesus first made a friend of every person He influenced. Our goal should be the same because, again, success is not about beating someone at a race or dominating others. It is about fulfilling our purpose by serving our gift to the world and by being a positive influence as we reflect the nature of God's kingdom on earth.

You can best serve someone's interests in life by being their friend. Solomon wrote, "Faithful are the wounds of a friend, but the kisses of an enemy are deceitful."[179] In other words, once you are someone's friend, if you correct them, they will thank you for it. If you're my friend, I will listen to you. If you're my friend, you will gain my confidence. I will open up to you; again, I will confide in you and tell you my reasons for doing what I do.

You make friends with people when you become interested in what they are interested in. I previously mentioned how Jesus met a woman at a well and asked her for some water. He knew that this woman had had five husbands and was hurting, but He didn't bring up any of that until after they had begun to talk and she was ready to hear what He had to say.

We need to be committed to people because it may take years for them to open up to us and respond to what we have to say. Most people are just looking for a friend. You don't confront people whom you want to help. You love them. Jesus said, "My command is this: Love each other as I have loved you. Greater love has no one than this: to lay down one's life for one's friends."[180] We need to work on laying down our life for people.

> *You can best serve someone's interests in life by being their friend. Solomon wrote, "Faithful are the wounds of a friend, but the kisses of an enemy are deceitful."*

MAINTAIN PERSONAL CHARACTER

One of the reasons I emphasized character in the previous section of this book is because character is the key to inspirational effectiveness. If we don't maintain good character, we jeopardize our influence. People need encouragement and positive influences if they are to fulfill their own purpose and live a peaceful, productive life. Remember, those who are successful serve other people; they don't push other people around. So, we must regularly ask ourselves, "Am I, in any way, violating the trust of those who have placed their faith in me? What impact am I having on those who are influenced or affected by my behavior?"

BECOME A TRANSFORMER

The above are all vital principles for being a positive influence in the lives of other people. There are many issues in our world, but each of us can begin to make a difference by starting in the domain of our gifting. We can build on our success by exercising our opportunity to influence others for good. As we do, we will not be mere observers of the world. We will be active, engaged transformers of our society.

CONCLUSION: COMPLETING YOUR PURPOSE

It's important for you to truly understand that your success is personal. It comes from accomplishing the purpose that you, as an individual, were put on this earth to fulfill. It comes from completing the assignment for which you were born. As we have seen, the journey of success begins when you discover and activate your inherent gift. Remember that you came to earth because you are "finished"—you arrived with everything you need to fulfill your purpose and be successful. Once you know your gift, your ability to succeed in life is a result of the decisions you make to manifest what is inside you. Keep in mind that success is not a pursuit but a result. You never have to worry about being successful—if you serve your gift to the world, you will succeed!

We have also seen how we can carry out our purpose and assignment only by following the laws and principles established in creation. These laws and principles are among the greatest discoveries we can make in life. Once you understand these laws, they're not difficult to put into practice. A person who knows and follows laws and principles will always be successful. Thus, the key to living effectively on this earth is a knowledge of laws, an understanding of laws, a submission to laws, and an application of laws.

When you obey laws, they will protect you. They will preserve you. They will sustain you. In the end, they will promote you. They will lead to your success and influence in the world.

Remember also that a fruit seed is successful only when it becomes a *fruit-bearing* tree. If such a seed becomes a tree alone, it is not yet successful. That tree must bear fruit, and the fruit must have seed within it as well. In other words, if you do only some of what you were meant to do in life, you haven't yet attained success. You have more of your assignment to fulfill. Thus, throughout your journey of success, endeavor to complete your purpose so that you will be able to say, as Paul of Tarsus did near the end of his life, "I have fought the good fight, I have finished the race, I have kept the faith."[181] In essence, Paul was saying, "There's nothing left for me to accomplish. I have done everything that I was sent here to do."

This brings us back to the top five questions in life:

1. Who am I?
2. Where am I from?
3. Why am I here?
4. What am I able to do?
5. Where am I going?

I hope that you are now closer to answering these questions for yourself. My purpose has been to equip you with the knowledge and practical principles necessary to experience personal development for success and influence. Put into practice what you have learned throughout this book. Make the choice to become all that you were meant to be.

NOTES

CHAPTER 1

1. John C. Maxwell, in "Overcoming the Leadership Development Myths We Tell Ourselves About Success," Maxwell Leadership, August 9, 2022, https://www.maxwellleadership.com/blog/success-myths/.

CHAPTER 2

2. Robert Louis Stevenson, *Familiar Studies of Men and Books* (New York: Charles Scribner's Sons, 1902), 167. With this statement, Stevenson is summarizing some of the views of Henry David Thoreau.
3. See Romans 3:4.

CHAPTER 3

4. Attributed to Allen Raine, *The Brooklyn Daily Eagle*, 1915. See QuoteResearch, "Quote Origin: As You Climb the Ladder of Success, Be Sure It's Leaning Against the Right Building," Quote Investigator, https://quoteinvestigator.com/2017/08/17/ladder/.
5. See, for example, Matthew 18:3.
6. See Exodus 3.
7. See 1 Kings 19:1–18.
8. Proverbs 18:16 (NKJV).
9. See John 8:32.
10. Pablo Picasso, "Pablo Picasso: Quotes," Goodreads, https://www.goodreads.com/quotes/203655-action-is-the-foundational-key-to-all-success.

CHAPTER 4

11. Warren Buffett, "Warren Buffett: Quotes," Goodreads, https://www.goodreads.com/author/quotes/756.Warren_Buffett.
12. Proverbs 23:4–5.
13. Merriam-Webster.com Dictionary, s.v. "obey," https://www.merriam-webster.com/dictionary/obey.
14. Galatians 6:7 (NASB).

CHAPTER 5

15. This quote is often attributed to Henry Ford. See, for example, "Success Quotes," Goodreads, https://www.goodreads.com/quotes/tag/success?page=6.
16. Genesis 1:26.
17. See Jeremiah 1:1–10.
18. Isaiah 46:10.
19. Psalm 37:4.
20. Isaiah 46:11.
21. Ecclesiastes 10:10.

CHAPTER 6

22. Matthew 13:11.
23. Matthew 16:19.
24. "2807. kleis," Bible Lexicon, Bible Hub, https://biblehub.com/greek/2807.htm.
25. Luke 11:52.
26. "Key," Easton's Bible Dictionary, Bible Study Tools, https://www.biblestudytools.com/dictionary/key/.
27. "8034. shem," Topical Lexicon, Bible Hub, https://biblehub.com/hebrew/8034.htm.
28. Exodus 3:14.
29. Psalm 119:98–100.

CHAPTER 7

30. Benjamin Disraeli, BrainyQuote, https://www.brainyquote.com/quotes/benjamin_disraeli_134331.
31. Matthew 5:17–18.
32. Verse 19.
33. Joshua 1:7–8.
34. Matthew 6:33.
35. Matthew 12:39.
36. See Matthew 4:5–6; Luke 4:9–11.
37. Matthew 4:7.
38. Matthew 6:12.
39. Jeremiah 29:11.
40. See John 10:17–18.
41. Proverbs 4:7.

CHAPTER 8

42. Isaac Newton, "Isaac Newton: Quotes," Goodreads, https://www.goodreads.com/author/quotes/135106.Isaac_Newton.
43. Genesis 2:16–17.
44. Romans 6:23.
45.Romans 6:23.
46. Merriam-Webster.com Dictionary, s.v. "law," https://www.merriam-webster.com/dictionary/law.
47. See Exodus 14:21–22.
48. See Matthew 14:22–23.
49. See John 8:31–32.
50. See John 15:5.
51. See Joshua 1:7–8.
52. NKJV.
53. Mark 4:26–28.
54. Jeremiah 31:33.

CHAPTER 9

55. Martin Luther King Jr., *Strength to Love* (Minneapolis, MN: Fortress Press, 2010), 26.
56. Matthew 5:20.
57. Matthew 15:2.
58. Verse 3.
59. Merriam-Webster.com Dictionary, s.v. "law," https://www.merriam-webster.com/dictionary/law.
60. Martin Luther King Jr., "Martin Luther King Jr. on Just and Unjust Laws," John F. Kennedy Presidential Library and Museum, https://www.jfklibrary.org/sites/default/files/2020-04/Birmingham%20Letter%20Excerpts%20for%20Activity.pdf.
61. Mark 9:23.
62. Mark 11:24–25.
63. Matthew 13:11.
64. Matthew 16:19.

CHAPTER 10

65. Proverbs 19:21.
66. Proverbs 19:21 (NKJV).
67. Hebrews 12:2 (NKJV).
68. See Genesis 37:1–11.
69. See Matthew 4:18–19 (NKJV).
70. See 1 Samuel 16:1–13.
71. See Genesis 12:1–5.

CHAPTER 11

72. John D. Rockefeller, "John D. Rockefeller Quotes," BrainyQuote, https://www.brainyquote.com/quotes/john_d_rockefeller_119902.

73. Amy Adkins, "Majority of U.S. Employees Not Engaged Despite Gains in 2014," Gallup, January 28, 2015, https://news.gallup.com/poll/181289/majority-employees-not-engaged-despite-gains-2014.aspx; Jim Harter, "U.S. Employee Engagement Sinks to 10-Year Low," Gallup, January 13, 2025, https://www.gallup.com/workplace/654911/employee-engagement-sinks-year-low.aspx.
74. See Genesis 3:17–19.
75. Genesis 2:15.
76. "Genesis 2:15," Interlinear Study Bible, StudyLight.org, https://www.studylight.org/interlinear-study-bible/greek/genesis/2-15.html.
77. Psalm 37:25.
78. John 4:34.
79. 2 Timothy 4:7.
80. John 19:30.
81. See, for example, John 15:19; 17:14–16.

CHAPTER 12

82. Theodore Roosevelt, *The Key to Success in Life* (New York: Federated Publishing Co., 1916), 12, Theodore Roosevelt Digital Library, Dickinson State University, https://www.theodorerooseveltcenter.org/Research/Digital-Library/Record/ImageViewer?libID=o283099&imageNo=5.
83. See Matthew 13:55; Mark 6:3.
84. Luke 2:49 (NKJV, KJV).
85. See John 4:34; 5:17; 10:37–38; 14:10.
86. Ecclesiastes 11:1.
87. Verse 2.
88. Verse 4.
89. Verses 5–6.
90. Proverbs 20:13.
91. Proverbs 18:16 (NKJV).

CHAPTER 13

92. Genesis 1:28. The word *replenish* is used in the King James Version.
93. Deuteronomy 8:17–18.
94. Deuteronomy 8:18.
95. Genesis 1:26 (NKJV).
96. Verse 26 (NKJV).
97. Verse 27 (NKJV).
98. Verse 28 (NKJV).
99. Verse 28 (NKJV).
100. "6509. parah," Topical Lexicon, Bible Hub, https://biblehub.com/hebrew/6509.htm.
101. Matthew 20:26–28.

CHAPTER 14

102. Jon M. Huntsman, *Winners Never Cheat: Even in Difficult Times* (Upper Saddle River, NJ: Pearson Education, Inc., 2014), 6.
103. Ecclesiastes 3:1 (NKJV).

104. See Daniel 3.
105. See Daniel 6.
106. William Shakespeare, *As You Like It*, ed. Agnes Latham (London: The Arden Shakespeare, 2005), 2.2.12. References are to act, scene, and line.
107. See Romans 8:28.
108. Proverbs 22:9.
109. Luke 6:38.
110. Psalm 106:1.
111. Jeremiah 29:11.
112. Matthew 6:33.
113. Luke 12:31–32.

CHAPTER 15

114. Steven R. Covey, *The 7 Habits of Highly Effective People: Powerful Lessons in Personal Change*, 25th Anniversary Edition (New York: Simon & Schuster, 2013), 110.
115. See Hebrews 11:1 (NKJV, KJV).
116. Proverbs 6:6–11.
117. Luke 6:41–42.
118. Psalm 119:45.

CHAPTER 16

119. Florence Nightingale, Gift Quotes, BrainyQuote, https://www.brainyquote.com/quotes/florence_nightingale_752508?src=t_gift.
120. Luke 14:28–30.
121. Proverbs 16:1.
122. Verse 9.
123. Proverbs 15:22.
124. Luke 11:5–10.
125. Merriam-Webster.com Dictionary, s.v. "persevere," https://www.merriam-webster.com/dictionary/persevere.
126. "Bahamas Wins Men's 4x400 Relay," Associated Press, August 10, 2012, reported by ESPN, https://www.espn.com/olympics/summer/2012/trackandfield/story/_/id/8257060/2012-london-olympics-bahamas-halts-us-streak-men-4x400-relay.
127. William Feather, "William Feather: Quotes," Goodreads, https://www.goodreads.com/quotes/346897-success-seems-to-be-largely-a-matter-of-hanging-on.
128. Isaiah 46:10.
129. Psalm 119:33–40.

CHAPTER 17

130. Theodore Roosevelt, Theodore Roosevelt Rotunda, American Museum of Natural History, https://www.amnh.org/exhibitions/permanent/theodore-roosevelt-memorial/roosevelt-rotunda.
131. Matthew 16:26.
132. Matthew 5:23–24.
133. See Matthew 5:43–45.
134. See, for example, Matthew 6:12; 18:21–35.

135. Genesis 1:28.
136. See Genesis 3.
137. James 3:11–12.
138. James 1:6–8.
139. Matthew 3:17.
140. John 10:30.
141. John 1:1–4, 14.
142. Colossians 2:9.
143. John 3:5.
144. See John 14:6.
145. Jeremiah 31:33.

CHAPTER 18

146. Matthew 6:21.
147. Proverbs 23:7 (NKJV).
148. Merriam-Webster.com Dictionary, s.v. "integrate," https://www.merriam-webster.com/dictionary/integrate.
149. *Online Etymology Dictionary*, http://www.etymonline.com/index.php?search=hypocrisy.
150. Proverbs 4:23.

CHAPTER 19

151. Albert Einstein, "Death of a Genius," *LIFE*, May 2, 1955, 64, https://books.google.com/books?id=dlYEAAAAMBAJ&q=%22man+of+value%22#v=snippet&q=%22man%20of%20value%22&.
152. Diaa Hadid, "First Jesus-Era House Found in Nazareth," NBC News, December 21, 2009, https://www.nbcnews.com/id/wbna34511072.
153. John 1:46.
154. John 6:42.
155. Luke 5:11. (See also verses 1–10.)
156. Matthew 8:27. (See also verses 23–26.)
157. See 1 Samuel 17:1–18:6.
158. Deuteronomy 8:18.
159. 1 Timothy 6:10.
160. See, for example, Genesis 12:1–3; 13.
161. See 1 Kings 3:5–15; 10:1–13, 23–24.
162. Numbers 13:33.
163. Winston S. Churchill, ed., *Never Give In!: The Best of Winston Churchill's Speeches* (New York: Hyperion, 2003), 229.
164. Dan Bilefsky and Jane Perlez, "Vaclav Havel, Former Czech President, Dies at 75," December 18, 2011, http://www.nytimes.com/2011/12/19/world/europe/vaclav-havel-dissident-playwright-who-led-czechoslovakia-dead-at-75.html.

CHAPTER 20

165. Booker T. Washington, *Up from Slavery* (Mineola, NY: Dover Publications, 1995), 35.

166. Merriam-Webster.com Dictionary, s.v. "culture," https://www.merriam-webster.com/dictionary/culture.
167. Genesis 2:8.
168. "5193. nata," Lexical Summary, Bible Hub, https://biblehub.com/hebrew/5193.htm.
169. See Genesis 1:27–28.
170. Attributed to J. D. Houston.
171. 1 Corinthians 9:22.
172. Proverbs 11:30.
173. 1 Corinthians 1:24, 30.
174. 1 Timothy 6:15–16.
175. John 1:14.
176. See John 4:1–42.
177. Matthew 10:16 (NKJV).
178. Proverbs 18:19 (NKJV).
179. Proverbs 27:6 (NKJV).
180. John 15:12–13.

CONCLUSION

181. 2 Timothy 4:7.

ABOUT THE AUTHOR

Dr. Myles Munroe (1954–2014) was an international motivational speaker, best-selling author, educator, leadership mentor, and consultant for government and business. Traveling extensively throughout the world, Dr. Munroe addressed critical issues affecting the full range of human, social, and spiritual development. He was a popular author of more than forty books, including *The Principles and Power of Vision, The Spirit of Leadership, Becoming a Leader, The Power of Character in Leadership, Understanding the Purpose and Power of Women, Understanding the Purpose and Power of Men,* and *Understanding the Purpose and Power of Prayer.*

Dr. Munroe was the founder and president of Bahamas Faith Ministries International (BFMI), a multidimensional organization headquartered in Nassau, Bahamas. He was the chief executive officer and chairman of the board of the International Third World Leaders Association and president of the International Leadership Training Institute.

Dr. Munroe earned B.A. and M.A. degrees from Oral Roberts University and the University of Tulsa and was awarded a number of honorary doctoral degrees. The parents of two adult children, Charisa and Chairo (Myles Jr.), Dr. Munroe and his wife, Ruth, traveled as a team and were involved in teaching seminars together. Both were leaders who ministered with sensitive hearts and international vision. In November 2014, they were tragically killed in an airplane crash en route to an annual leadership conference sponsored by Bahamas Faith Ministries International. A statement from Dr. Munroe in his book *The Power of Character in Leadership* summarizes his own legacy: "Remember that character ensures the longevity of leadership, and men and women of principle will leave important legacies and be remembered by future generations."

The legacy of Dr. Myles Munroe is carried on today by Munroe Global Inc. and Munroe Group of Companies Ltd.

Visit www.munroeglobal.com.